Modern Critical Views

Modern Critical Views

Katherine Mansfield
Christopher Marlowe
Andrew Marvell
Herman Melville
George Meredith
James Merrill
John Stuart Mill
Arthur Miller
Henry Miller
John Milton
Yukio Mishima
Molière
Michel de Montaigne
Eugenio Montale
Marianne Moore
Alberto Moravia
Toni Morrison
Alice Munro
Iris Murdoch
Robert Musil
Vladimir Nabokov
V. S. Naipaul
R. K. Narayan
Pablo Neruda
John Henry Newman
Friedrich Nietzsche
Frank Norris
Joyce Carol Oates
Sean O'Casey
Flannery O'Connor
Christopher Okigbo
Charles Olson
Eugene O'Neill
José Ortega y Gasset
Joe Orton
George Orwell
Ovid
Wilfred Owen
Amos Oz
Cynthia Ozick
Grace Paley
Blaise Pascal
Walter Pater
Octavio Paz
Walker Percy
Petrarch
Pindar
Harold Pinter
Luigi Pirandello
Sylvia Plath
Plato

Plautus
Edgar Allan Poe
Poets of Sensibility & the
  Sublime
Poets of the Nineties
Alexander Pope
Katherine Anne Porter
Ezra Pound
Anthony Powell
Pre-Raphaelite Poets
Marcel Proust
Manuel Puig
Alexander Pushkin
Thomas Pynchon
Francisco de Quevedo
François Rabelais
Jean Racine
Ishmael Reed
Adrienne Rich
Samuel Richardson
Mordecai Richler
Rainer Maria Rilke
Arthur Rimbaud
Edwin Arlington Robinson
Theodore Roethke
Philip Roth
Jean-Jacques Rousseau
John Ruskin
J. D. Salinger
Jean-Paul Sartre
Gershom Scholem
Sir Walter Scott
William Shakespeare
  Histories & Poems
  Comedies & Romances
  Tragedies
George Bernard Shaw
Mary Wollstonecraft
  Shelley
Percy Bysshe Shelley
Sam Shepard
Richard Brinsley Sheridan
Sir Philip Sidney
Isaac Bashevis Singer
Tobias Smollett
Alexander Solzhenitsyn
Sophocles
Wole Soyinka
Edmund Spenser
Gertrude Stein
John Steinbeck

Stendhal
Laurence Sterne
Wallace Stevens
Robert Louis Stevenson
Tom Stoppard
August Strindberg
Jonathan Swift
John Millington Synge
Alfred, Lord Tennyson
William Makepeace Thackeray
Dylan Thomas
Henry David Thoreau
James Thurber and S. J.
  Perelman
J. R. R. Tolkien
Leo Tolstoy
Jean Toomer
Lionel Trilling
Anthony Trollope
Ivan Turgenev
Mark Twain
Miguel de Unamuno
John Updike
Paul Valéry
Cesar Vallejo
Lope de Vega
Gore Vidal
Virgil
Voltaire
Kurt Vonnegut
Derek Walcott
Alice Walker
Robert Penn Warren
Evelyn Waugh
H. G. Wells
Eudora Welty
Nathanael West
Edith Wharton
Patrick White
Walt Whitman
Oscar Wilde
Tennessee Williams
William Carlos Williams
Thomas Wolfe
Virginia Woolf
William Wordsworth
Jay Wright
Richard Wright
William Butler Yeats
A. B. Yehoshua
Emile Zola

Modern Critical Views

H. D.

Edited and with an introduction by
Harold Bloom
Sterling Professor of the Humanities
Yale University

CHELSEA HOUSE PUBLISHERS
New York ◇ Philadelphia

Printed and bound in the United States of America

10 9 8 7 6 5 4 3 2 1

∞ The paper used in this publication meets the minimum
requirements of the American National Standard for Permanence
of Paper for Printed Library Materials, Z39.48–1984.

Library of Congress Cataloging-in-Publication Data
H. D. / edited and with an introduction by Harold Bloom.
   p.   cm.—(Modern critical views)
   Bibliography: p.
   Includes index.
   Summary: A collection of nine critical essays on the American
poet and novelist, arranged in chronological order of their
original publication.
   ISBN 1-55546-319-3 : $19.95
   1. H. D. (Hilda Doolittle), 1886–1961—Criticism and
interpretation. [1. H. D. (Hilda Doolittle), 1886–1961—
Criticism and interpretation. 2. American literature—History
and criticism.] I. Bloom, Harold. II. Title: H.D. III. Series.
PS3507.O726Z69 1988
811'.52—dc19   87–18342
                                               CIP
                                               AC

Contents

Editor's Note

This volume brings together a representative selection of the best criticism available upon the poetry of H. D. (Hilda Doolittle). The critical essays are reprinted here in the chronological order of their original publication. I am grateful to Susanna Gilbert for her assistance in editing this volume.

My introduction centers upon "The Master" and "The Poet," somewhat pre-Raphaelite verse tributes to Freud and to D. H. Lawrence, respectively. The chronological sequence of criticism begins with the poet Denise Levertov's appreciation of H. D., and then continues with the ego psychologist-critic Norman N. Holland's exposition of the relation of H. D.'s prose *Tribute to Freud* to her literary myth.

The question of style in H. D.'s novels is discussed by A. Kingsley Weatherhead, while Susan Friedman offers a feminist defense of H. D.'s achievement. Susan Gubar, one of our leading feminist critics, gives a reading of H. D.'s *Trilogy,* after which Louis L. Martz achieves a memorable overview of the major phases of H. D.'s poetic career.

Adalaide Morris relates H. D.'s visionary powers in her poems to the psychic defense that Freud called "projection," while Albert Gelpi concerns himself with the major long poem, *Helen in Egypt.* In this book's concluding essay, the poet Robert Duncan conveys the quality of H. D.'s artistry, in a tribute made all the more valuable by the authentic continuity between H. D.'s poetry and Duncan's.

Introduction

Like Ezra Pound, her close friend and poetic colleague, H. D. seems to me essentially an American pre-Raphaelite poet, a naming that I intend as a compliment since I deeply love the poetry of the Rossettis, Morris, Meredith, and Swinburne. Even as Pound assimilates Dante Gabriel Rossetti to Walt Whitman, so H. D. compounds Christina Rossetti with Emily Dickinson, and both together with the male sequence of Dante Gabriel Rossetti, William Morris, Pound, and D. H. Lawrence.

Louis L. Martz, in his "Introduction" to H. D.'s *The Collected Poems 1912–1944,* sensitively sketches the relation between the psychosexual and the poetic crises that kept her from publishing any volumes of poetry between 1931 and 1944. Her brief analysis with Freud himself (about three months in 1933, and some five weeks in 1934) issued not only in her *Tribute to Freud* but in a number of fairly strong if problematic poems, three in particular, which Martz reports she grouped in the order of "The Dancer," "The Master," and "The Poet." "The Dancer" is the most problematic of these and perhaps would not matter much, except that it informs a powerful return of its central trope in the midst of "The Master," which is a moving tribute to Freud. Martz shrewdly calls "The Poet" a calm and measured tribute to D. H. Lawrence, and while it is not as distinguished a poem as "The Master," it has its own value and place in H. D.'s achievement.

Tribute to Freud is a rather overpraised book, particularly dear to Freudian literalists from Ernest Jones to the present since it is a kind of hagiography. H. D. herself chats on rapturously, while the old Professor somehow never does get to say anything remotely memorable. Precisely how he clarifies either the poet's bisexuality or her creative inhibitions may escape even the most assiduous and skilled reader. Section 10 of "Writing on the Wall," the first part of the *Tribute,* is both famous and typical:

So much for the Princess, Hanns Sachs, and Walter Schmideberg,

1

the one-time Rittmeister of the 15th Imperial Austro-Hungarian
Hussars of His Royal Highness, Archduke Francis Salvator. For
myself, I veer round, uncanonically seated stark upright with my
feet on the floor. The Professor himself is uncanonical enough;
he is beating with his hand, with his fist, on the head-piece of
the old-fashioned horsehair sofa that had heard more secrets than
the confession box of any popular Roman Catholic father-con-
fessor in his heyday. This was the homely historical instrument
of the original scheme of psychotherapy, of psychoanalysis, the
science of the unravelling of the tangled skeins of the unconscious
mind and the healing implicit in the process. *Consciously,* I was
not aware of having said anything that might account for the
Professor's outburst. And even as I veered around, facing him,
my mind was detached enough to wonder if this was some idea
of *his* for speeding up the analytic content or redirecting the flow
of associated images. The Professor said, "The trouble is—I am
an old man—*you do not think it worth your while to love me.*"

("Writing on the Wall")

Presumably such a shock tactic was intended to speed up the transference, but if Freud actually said anything like this, then he was mistaken, as
clearly H. D. loved him beyond measure. "But the Professor insisted I myself
wanted to be Moses; not only did I want to be a boy but I wanted to be a
hero." That certainly sounds like Freud, or by now like a self-parody on his
part. There is something quaintly archaic about *Tribute to Freud,* where the
Professor's interventions are so accurate, his spiritual efficacy so instanta-
neous, as to suggest the advent of a new age of faith, the Freud era. A prose
memorial provokes our resistances when it seems too pious or too amiably
earnest. The pre-Raphaelite aura, hieratic and isolated, with its characteristic
effect of a hard-edged phantasmagoria, rescues "The Master" from the cloy-
ing literalism of the *Tribute.* "The old man" of the poem is God's prophet,
since "the dream is God," and Freud therefore is heard as one who speaks
with authority: "his command / was final" and "his tyranny was absolute, /
for I had to love him then." The command, at least as H. D. interpreted it,
was to accept her own bisexuality as being one with her poethood:

> I do not know what to say to God,
> for the hills
> answer his nod,
> and the sea
> when he tells his daughter,

white Mother
of green
leaves
and green rills
and silver,
to still
tempest
or send peace
and surcease of peril
when a mountain has spit fire:

I did not know how to differentiate
between volcanic desire,
anemones like embers
and purple fire
of violets
like red heat,
and the cold
silver
of her feet:

I had two loves separate;
God who loves all mountains,
alone knew why
and understood
and told the old man
to explain

the impossible,

which he did.

("The Master")

The phallic or volcanic is evidently preferred by this male God, at least rhetorically, but of the "two loves separate" the "cold / silver / of her feet" triumphs with the re-entry of the dancer in section 5. The force that comes with celebration of the dancer depends upon H. D.'s vision of herself as wrestling Jacob, arguing till daybreak, and of Freud as God or His angel, giving further rhetorical primacy to "the man-strength" rather than to the dancer's leapings:

I was angry with the old man
with his talk of the man-strength,

I was angry with his mystery, his mysteries,
I argued till day-break;

O, it was late,
and God will forgive me, my anger,
but I could not accept it.

I could not accept from wisdom
what love taught,
woman is perfect.

("The Dancer")

That would appear to have meant that a woman's bisexuality or her perfection (in the sense of completeness) was of a different and more acceptable order than a man's bisexuality. The ecstasy of section 5 gently mocks the Freudian "man-strength" even as it salutes the dancer for needing no male, since at least as dancer (or poet) woman is indeed pragmatically perfect. Section 5 has a kind of uncanny force, akin to Yeatsian celebrations of the dancer as image. But the authentic strength of the poem centers elsewhere, in its elegiac identifications of the dead father, Freud, with the earth, and with all the dead fathers. Freud is Saturn, ancient wisdom, and the rock that cannot be broken—a new earth. His temples will be everywhere, yet H. D. cries out: "only I, I will escape," an escape sanctioned by Freud as the freedom of the woman poet. Though D. H. Lawrence is not even alluded to in "The Master," he enters the poem by negation, since it is transformed into a fierce hymn against Lawrence's vision of sexual release:

no man will be present in those mysteries,
yet all men will kneel,
no man will be potent,
important,
yet all men will feel
what it is to be a woman,
will yearn,
burn,
turn from easy pleasure
to hardship
of the spirit,

men will see how long they have been blind,
poor men
poor man-kind

how long
how long
this thought of the man-pulse has tricked them.
has weakened them,
shall see woman,
perfect.

("The Master")

The blindness is precisely Lawrence's in H. D.'s judgment, and it is
hinted at, in muted form, in "The Poet," not so much an elegy for Lawrence
as for her failed friendship with him. What seems clear is that her sexual
self-acceptance, whether Freudian or not, gave her the creative serenity that
made possible the wonderfully controlled, hushed resignation of her wisely
limited farewell to Lawrence:

No,
I don't pretend, in a way, to understand,
nor know you,
nor even see you;

I say,
"I don't grasp his philosophy,
and I don't understand,"

but I put out a hand, touch a cold door,
(we have both come from so far);
I touch something imperishable;
I think,
why should he stay there?
why should he guard a shrine so alone,
so apart,
on a path that leads nowhere?

he is keeping a candle burning in a shrine
where nobody comes,
there must be some mystery
in the air
about him,

he couldn't live alone in the desert,
without vision to comfort him,

there must be voices somewhere.
                                        ("The Poet")

The wistfulness of that tribute, if it is a tribute, veils the harshness of the critique. A woman can be perfect, but a man cannot, though Lawrence would not learn this. One can imagine his response to H. D.; it would have been violent, but that perhaps would have confirmed her stance, whether sanctioned or unsanctioned by her father and master, Freud.

DENISE LEVERTOV

H. D.: An Appreciation

Like so many others, I was for years familiar only with a handful of H. D.'s
early poems. "Peartree," "Orchard," "Heat," "Oread." Beautiful though
they were, they did not lead me to look further, at the time. Perhaps it was
that being such absolutes of their kind they seemed final, the end of some
road not mine; and I was looking for doors, ways in, tunnels through.

When I came, late, to her later work, not searching but by inevitable
chance, what I found was precisely doors, ways in, tunnels through. One of
these later poems, "The Moon in Your Hands," says:

> If you take the moon in your hands
> and turn it round
> (heavy slightly tarnished platter)
> you're there;

This was to find not a finality but a beginning. The poem ends with that
sense of beginning:

> when my soul turned round,
> perceiving the other-side of everything,
> mullein-leaf, dogwood-leaf, moth-wing
> and dandelion-seed under the ground.

It was not until after the publication, in *Evergreen Review* no. 5, of her
poem *Sagesse* that I read the great War Trilogy. In *Sagesse* the photograph

---

From *Poetry* 100, no. 3 (June 1962). © 1962 by Denise Levertov Goodman.

of an owl—a White Faced Scops Owl from Sierra Leone, which is reproduced along with the poem—starts a train of thought and feeling which leads poet and reader far back into childhood, by way of word origins and word-sound associations, and back again to a present more resonant, more full of possibilities and subtle awareness, because of that journey. The interpenetration of past and present, of mundane reality and intangible reality, is typical of H. D. For me this poem (written in 1957) was an introduction to the world of the Trilogy—*The Walls Do Not Fall* (1944), *Tribute to the Angels* (1945), *The Flowering of the Rod* (1946). These were an experience life had been storing for me until I was ready to begin to receive it. (For I had been in London myself throughout the period when these books were being written and published, and had, as I came to recall, even "seen"—without seeing—those parts of them that appeared, before book publication, in *Life and Letters Today.* But I had been too young to know them; just as I was too young—younger than my years—to *experience,* as a poet, the bombing of London: I lived in the midst of it but in a sense it did not *happen* to me, and though my own first book, in 1946, was written during that time, the war appeared in it only offstage or as the dark background of adolescent anxiety.)

What was it I discovered, face to face at last with the great poetry of H. D.'s maturity? What was—is—the core of the experience? I think this is it: that the icily passionate precision of the earlier work, the "Greek" vision, had not been an *end,* a closed achievement, but a preparation: so that all the strength built up, poem by poem, as if in the bones, in the remorseless clear light of that world—

>Great, bright portal,
>shelf of rock,
>rocks fitted in long ledges,
>rocks fitted to dark, to silver granite,
>to lighter rock—
>clean cut, white against white—

was *there,* there to carry darkness and mystery and the questions behind questions when she came to that darkness and those questions. She showed a way to penetrate mystery; which means, not to flood darkness with light so that darkness is destroyed, but to *enter into* darkness, mystery, so that it is experienced. And by *darkness* I don't mean *evil;* not evil but the Other Side, the Hiddenness before which man must shed his arrogance; Sea out of which the first creeping thing and Aphrodite emerge; Cosmos in which the little speck of the earth whirls, and in the earth "the dandelion seed."

"Sirius:
what mystery is this?

you are seed,
corn near the sand,
enclosed in black-lead,
ploughed land.

Sirius:
what mystery is this?

you are drowned
in the river;
the spring freshets
push open the water-gates.

Sirius:
what mystery is this?

where heat breaks, and cracks
the sand-waste,
you are a mist
of snow: white, little flowers.

The "style"—or since style too often means *manner,* I would rather say the *mode,* the means—is invisible: or no, not invisible but transparent, something one both sees and sees through, like handblown glass of the palest smoke-color or the palest water-green. And in this transparent mode H. D. spoke of essentials. It is a simplicity not of reduction but of having gone further, further out of the circle of known light, further in towards an unknown center. Whoever wishes a particular example, let him read part VI of *The Walls Do Not Fall*—the part beginning:

> In me (the worm) clearly
> is no righteousness, but this—.

I would like to quote the whole; but it is too long; and it is such a marvelous musical whole that I cannot bear to quote fragments. It can be found in the Grove Press *Selected Poems of H. D.* (1957).

After I had begun to know the later poems I returned to the *Collected Poems* of 1925 and saw them anew. "The great, bright portal . . . clean cut, white against white" was not the dominant I had thought it. The poems I had thought of as shadowless were full of shadows, planes, movement: correspondences with what was to come. But I, and perhaps others of my generation, could come to realize this only through a knowledge of the after-work.

About a year and a half before her death I had the privilege of meeting H. D. (and thereafter exchanging some letters with her until the stroke which began her last illness broke off communication). The woman of whom Horace Gregory has written that he could distinguish her from far off in a crowd by her tall grace, was old and badly crippled; but full of eager life. Yet even though her novel, *Bid Me to Live,* was newly published, and she had just received the Gold Medal for Poetry of the Academy of Arts and Letters, there were at that time many, alas, who believed her dead, and who dismissed her as "one of the Imagistes—a poet of that period." So little was her most important poetry read and recognized for the great work it is, that my homage and Robert Duncan's seemed to be a surprise to her, and to move her in a way deeply moving to us. She herself had at the time of my second meeting with her been reading some of the youngest young poets; and how quick she was to respond to what she found there of life, of energy.

There is no poet from whom one can learn more about precision; about the music, the play of sound, that arises miraculously out of fidelity to the truth of experience; about the possibility of the disappearance, in the crucible, of *manner.*

She wrote much that has not been published. Her last book, *Helen in Egypt,* the publication of which almost coincided with her death, is (like *Bid Me to Live* in its different form) a world which one may enter if one will; a life-experience that gives rise to changes in the reader, small at first, but who knows how far-reaching. The alternations, in *Helen,* of prose and poetry are not alternations of flatness and intensity but of contrasted tone, as in a Bach cantata the vocal parts are varied by the sinfonias, and each illumines and complements the other. *Bid Me to Live* and *Helen in Egypt* are neither of them works to be idly dipped into: one must go inside and live in them, live them through.

Indeed, this is true of all her work: the more one reads it, the more it yields. It is poetry both "pure" and "engaged"; attaining its purity—that is, its unassailable identity as word-music, the music of word-sounds and the rhythmic structure built of them—through its very engagement, its concern with matters of the greatest importance to everyone: the life of the soul, the interplay of psychic and material life.

NORMAN N. HOLLAND

Tribute to Freud *and the H. D. Myth*

H. D. wrote *Tribute to Freud* almost like a psychoanalysis itself, as a series of free associations, letting her thoughts lead her where they would. The associations are not entirely free, however; she omits so as to protect her privacy. H. D. says almost nothing about her contemporary life and very little about her adult life at all. She is completely silent on matters of adult sexuality (although it is clear that she and Freud worked with infantile sexual material). Instead, she produces a whole series of mythological associations. Most of the time she relies without explanation on connotations and verbal echoes in her own and, particularly, in Freud's phrasings. Only once does she make a straightforward interpretation. We, her readers, are left to make the connections ourselves, though the connections are there to be made, at least for her developmental years.

Because she wrote in a series of free associations, the book became a seamless web: to pick up any one point is to involve oneself in all. Perhaps the best way to give the material sequence is to follow out Freud's changing roles. One would expect H. D. (or any other analysand) in the transference situation of psychoanalysis to transfer or project onto the analyst her positive and negative feelings toward the key figures of her childhood—her mother, her father, and, in H. D.'s case, the brother who was so singularly important to her. In seeking, then, the common source in childhood of H. D.'s life-style and her literary style, we can use Freud himself, as he is assigned various roles in the transference, for our Ariadne thread.

From *Contemporary Literature* 10, no. 4 (Autumn 1969). © 1969 by the Board of Regents of the University of Wisconsin System.

We can enter the labyrinth with H. D. herself, for "Undoubtedly," she noted, "the Professor took an important clue from the first reaction of a new analysand or patient." When first she entered his consulting-room, Freud stood waiting for the tall, shy woman of forty-seven to speak. H. D., however, silently took an inventory of the contents of the room, Freud's collection of Greek and Egyptian antiquities. Finally, "waiting and finding that I would not or could not speak, he uttered. What he said—and I thought a little sadly—was, 'You are the only person who has ever come into this room and looked at the things in the room before looking at me.'" The Professor might have taken a clue to H. D.'s tendency to approach someone she desired through an intermediary, particularly a mythological object or symbol.

The first such intermediary in the book is "the Flying Dutchman." J. J. van der Leeuw, so nicknamed because he flew his own plane. "His soul fitted his body," wrote H. D., and she surely had not forgotten when she wrote, much later in the book, of her own soul, "Its body did not fit it very well." H. D.'s only contact with van der Leeuw was that, one day, "We had exchanged 'hours,'" and perhaps her quotation marks suggest that she recognized the pun on *ours*. When H. D. heard that he had crashed his plane and died in Tanganyika, she rushed back to Vienna to express her sorrow and sympathy for Freud. "'You have come,'" he bluntly interpreted, "'to take his place.'" Indeed, she speaks of van der Leeuw as her "brother-in-arms" and Mercury.

Her brother was in arms when he was killed in France in 1918, and H. D. herself links soldier and airman when she has her mystical vision at Corfu or when she numbers her brother among the "poised, disciplined and valiant young winged Mercuries" who fell from the air during the war. Freud's remark "that the analysand who preceded me [van der Leeuw] was 'actually considerably taller'" than H. D. leads her directly to a statement and a memory, "My brother is considerably taller."

Though she does not even give us his name, this older brother was obviously a key figure in H. D.'s childhood, for he "is admittedly his mother's favourite." H. D. loved and admired him, too, but she also envied him: ". . . I was not, they said, pretty and I was not, it was very easy to see, quaint and quick and clever like my brother. My brother? Am I my brother's keeper?" And perhaps she did feel like Cain, even when she most treasured and preserved her slain brother's memory (as in the "undisciplined thoughts" of this passage)—or when they were children together.

Yet that very brother seemed to be the intermediary through whom she could reach her distant mother: "The trouble is, she knows so many people and they come and interrupt. And besides that, she likes my brother better.

If I stay with my brother, become part almost of my brother, perhaps I can get nearer to *her*."

Thus, her brother becomes the first of many mythological lover-heroes in H. D.'s quests: Perseus, Hermes, the Flying Dutchman, the Professor(s)— in Norman Holmes Pearson's apt phrase, "the one searched for (who himself searches)." They are mythological twins, like Little-Brother, Little-Sister in Grimm, the twin brother-sister of the Nile, or Castor and Pollux (but, as she writes this, H. D. corrects the gender, adding Helen and Clytaemnestra). "One is sometimes the shadow of the other; often one is lost and the one seeks the other. . . ."

H. D. herself tells us that what she sought in her brother was to get closer to her mother. A memory of him, however, suggests another *motif*. He had taken one of the "sacred objects" from his father's desk, a magnifying glass, and was showing his sister how he could focus the sunlight to burn a piece of paper. His father sternly told him to stop, pointing out his double crime, that he had done something like play with matches and that he had taken something from the study table. Possibly, to become one with her brother meant to acquire the special powers that men seemed to have, the power to bring fire from heaven like Prometheus, to understand the mysterious symbols her astronomer-father used or her brother's larger vocabulary, to be "quaint and clever" instead of "not very advanced," perhaps most important, to have arrived first, to be older, to be not a foreigner or "a little stranger." All these things might be possible with a boy's body instead of a girl's. As she puts it in an enigmatic comment, left to stand by itself after a story about her brother and discoveries under a log, "There were things under things, as well as things inside things."

H. D. suggests still another goal she sought in her brother, another memory, the wish that she could be a mother: perhaps her brother could be her doll's father, perhaps her own father could be. She would be the virgin mother, "building a dream and the dream is symbolized by the . . . doll in her arms." To Freud, in the transference, she brought all these fantasies and investments of her brother, just as she brought the dreams concretized as the doll.

Freud is Saint Michael, who will slay the dragon of her fears, but Michael was also regent of the planet Mercury—"in Renaissance paintings, we are not surprised to see Saint Michael wearing the winged sandals and sometimes even the winged helmet of the classic messenger of the Gods." Thus there are associations: "Thoth, Hermes, Mercury, and last Michael, Captain or Centurion of the hosts of heaven."

When she compares Freud to the Centurion of heaven, she cannot have forgotten that ten pages earlier, she had said that, in his refusal to accept her notions of immortality, his slamming the door on visions of the future, he was standing "like the Roman Centurion before the gate at Pompeii, who did not move from his station before the gateway since he had received no orders to do so, and who stood for later generations to wonder at, embalmed in hardened lava, preserved in the very fire and ashes that had destroyed him." She goes on to quote Freud, " 'At least, they have not burnt me at the stake.' " Earlier, she had been grateful that the Professor had not lived until World War II. ". . . He was a handful of ashes" "before the blast and bombing and fires had devastated this city. . . ." The wish is kindly meant, but underneath, it shows the same ambivalence as toward that other Mercury, her brother.

Freud, like Prometheus, like her brother, had stolen fire from heaven, from the sun. He, too, was not only the victim, but the cause of explosions: "Many of his words did, in a sense, explode . . . opening up mines of hidden treasures." More gently, after an especially striking insight, he would say, " 'Ah—now—we must celebrate *this*' "; he would rise, select, light, and then, "from the niche [where he sat rose] the smoke of burnt incense, the smouldering of his mellow, fragrant cigar."

She identified Freud with Asklepios, the "blameless physician," son of the sun god Apollo. "He was the son of the sun, Phoebos Apollo, and music and medicine were alike sacred to this source of light." "And here was the master-musician, he, too, a son of Apollo, who would harmonize the whole human spirit. . . ." She identifies herself as a fellow-servant of Apollo, the Priestess or Pythoness of Delphi; thus she suggests that Freud is her peer and brother. But by punning on "son" and "sun," she makes Apollo himself, the father, the "son." It is well to remember her father was another "Professor."

In short, Freud has come to stand for the whole ambiguous network of wishes and relationships associated with the oedipal wishes of a little girl: that she could become a mother with her brother as father; that she could, by marrying her father, become her brother's mother; that she could, by marrying her brother, become her father's mother. She seems to recognize these ambiguities when she calls Freud "the Old Man of the Sea," Proteus, the shapeshifter, or compares him to two-faced Janus, who leads her to Thoth, Hermes, Mercury, and finally the Flying Dutchman. But Janus is also Captain January, a beloved old lighthouse keeper who takes in a shipwrecked child. Freud becomes in the transference not only her brother but also her father. This dual relationship with Freud matches H. D.'s extended identification of herself with Mignon, the boy-girl, from *Wilhelm Meister*, who is both sister but also would-be sexual object to the hero.

Even so, in the strangely labile world of a psychoanalysis, Freud can become H. D.'s father, but so can H. D. She herself makes the connection: her father, being an astronomer, often slept on a couch in his study during the day, and she was not to disturb him. "But now it is I who am lying on the couch in the room lined with books." Her father had in his study a "white owl under a bell-jar"; she has the Professor, sitting "there quietly, like an old owl in a tree." (And, one should remember, the owl is an emblem for Athené with whom H. D. identified herself.) At the top of the astronomical tables he made up, her father would write something which was neither a letter nor a number: "he will sketch in a hieroglyph; it may stand for one of the Houses or Signs of the Zodiac, or it may be a planet simply: Jupiter or Mars or Venus." Dreams, visions, and all the shapes, lines, and graphs she speaks of are "the *hieroglyph of the unconscious*" (H. D.'s italics). As for herself, "Niké, Victory seemed to be the clue, seemed to be my own special sign or part of my hieroglyph." Similarly, in *Helen in Egypt* Helen's body becomes the hieroglyph: "She herself is the writing." If one is a writing, one is looked at—by Freud, by the aloof father, perhaps even by the distant mother.

Later H. D. will identify herself with Freud by seeing *him* as victorious, but at the moment we are concerned with Freud's becoming, in the transference, H. D.'s father. Obviously, the bearded seventy-seven-year-old physician more easily suggested a father-figure than a gallant, winged Mercury, particularly when he listed off his grandchildren as his claim to immortality. On at least one occasion, H. D. felt with Freud "like a child, summoned to my father's study or my mother's sewing-room or told by a teacher to wait in after school. . . ." The time Freud seemed to lose his temper, "it was as if the Supreme Being had hammered with his fist on the back of the couch . . . ," but it was also (in the fluid world of transferences) "like a child hammering a porridge-spoon on the table."

Freud reminded H. D. of her father, however, in more specific ways than as an authority-figure. For one thing, he seemed able to persist. Her father had died at the shock of learning of her brother's death, while "The Professor had shock upon shock. But he had not died." Another line of association leads to what men have and what doctors do: "my father possessed sacred symbols . . . he, like the Professor, had old, old sacred objects on his study table." In his study, her father had a photograph of Rembrandt's *The Anatomy Lesson,* and her father identified his forebears with the Puritans— "Their hats were like the hats the doctors wore . . . ," and indeed he rather liked to identify himself with doctors. Further, "A doctor has a bag with strange things in it, steel and knives and scissors." Doctors know secrets.

Her father "entrusts" her with his paper-knife to cut the pages of some of his journals. "The half-naked man on the table was dead so it did not hurt him when the doctors sliced his arm with a knife or a pair of scissors." She sees psychoanalysis as a special form of Socratic method and Socratic method in turn as fencing. Freud, in the transference, has acquired both phallic power and the power to cut.

She speaks of the Tree of Knowledge: "His [Freud's] were the great giant roots of that tree, but mine, with hair-like almost invisible feelers. . . . the invisible intuitive rootlet. . . . the smallest possible subsoil rootlet" could also solve mysteries. One of the difficulties, Freud noted about this time, in the analysis of a woman is "that her strongest motive in coming for treatment was the hope that, after all, she might still obtain a male organ, the lack of which was so painful to her [in "Analysis Terminable and Interminable"]." We should bear in mind this belief (that the analyst—the doctor—will restore what has been, in fantasy, cut off) in considering Freud's interpretive "gifts" to H. D.

One day he led her from the couch into his study to show her one of his Greek figurines: "'*This* is my favourite,' he said," and he held out a little bronze Pallas Athené. "'She is perfect,' he said, '*only she has lost her spear*'" (H. D.'s italics). H. D. remembered that Athené's winged form was Niké, so that this was a Niké without wings, Niké A-pteros, as, for example, H. D. had seen her in Athens (made so that Victory would never fly away to another city). She meditates on "She is perfect." ". . . The little bronze statue was a perfect symbol, made in man's image (in woman's, as it happened), to be venerated as a projection of abstract thought, Pallas Athené . . . sprung full-armed from the head of her father, our-father, Zeus. . . ."

Maybe it wasn't a spear she had been holding—"It might have been a rod or staff." H. D. had been remembering Aaron's rod which turned into a living reptile; Moses, Adam and Eve; the Tree of Life cursed so that it would bring forth only thistles, related to a vision of hers in adolescence of a thistle and a serpent inscribed on a stone. Seal, symbol, serpent, signet, Sigmund—all these *s*'s remind her of the question marks that surrounded her mystical vision on Corfu. The serpent makes her think of Asklepios, the serpent being the sign of healing and wisdom and rebirth. There was a serpent crouched at the feet of Athené.

"It might have been a rod or staff," and she goes on to remember the occasion when the Professor gave her a little branch from a box of oranges his son had sent. In effect, Freud was giving her symbolically what Freud felt every woman patient wanted. She herself could associate to that golden bough another gift or compliment Freud gave her: "There are very few who understand this [that "my discoveries are a basis for a very grave philosophy"], *there are very few who are capable of understanding this*" (H. D.'s italics). Freud was, in effect, giving H. D. back the understanding that leads to victory, the masculine power represented in sacred objects, the ability to live in her wingless self, all of which, at some level of her being, H. D. felt, her real father had taken away. Or, perhaps, her mother had never given her.

From psychoanalytic theory, one would expect the father to inherit the conflicts and feelings associated with the mother. Indeed, H. D. is quite explicit about this: "*If* one could stay near her always, there would be no break in consciousness—but half a loaf is better than no bread and there are things, not altogether negligible, to be said for *him*." Thus, on the occasion when her brother took the magnifying glass, "Our father came down the steps. This picture could be found in an old collection of Bible illustrations. . . ." We are hearing a verbal echo of what H. D. and Freud called "the dream of the Princess." A mysterious, beautiful Egyptian lady is coming down a flight of steps. "I, the dreamer, wait at the foot of the steps. . . . There, in the water beside me, is a shallow basket or ark or box or boat" containing a baby which, of course, the Princess must find, protect, and shelter. This is, obviously, the Doré illustration, *Moses in the Bulrushes,* and H. D. is perhaps the baby or perhaps the child Miriam half concealed in the rushes. "Do I wish myself, in the deepest unconscious or subconscious layers of my being, to be the founder of a new religion?" These religious wishes were her one point of difference with Freud: "About the greater transcendental issues, we never argued. But there was an argument implicit in our very bones." It was in this context that she cast him as the burnt centurion.

"We touched lightly on some of the more abstruse transcendental problems, it is true, but we related them to the familiar family-complex." "A Queen or Princess," she notes, "is obvious mother-symbol . . . ," but equally obviously her need for a religious level of being (and, clearly, psychoanalysis provided one outlet for her need to have faith in something) does not simply come down to her wish to become a "Princess" or "prophetess." Participation in another level of being makes her a mother in a far more powerful sense. She can restore her own lost ones, for "The dead were living in so far as they lived in memory or were recalled in dream."

Further, we can look at the wish for an eternal order from the point of view not of the child wishing to become the mother, but of the child wishing to be mothered. That other level of reality implies a being who is always there. The analyst never dies or goes away: ". . . I looked at the things in his room before I looked at him; for I knew the things in his room were symbols of Eternity and contained him then, as Eternity contains him now." When

Freud one day spoke as though his only immortality lay in his grandchildren, "I was deeply distressed," "It worried me. . . ." ". . . I felt a sudden gap, a severance, a chasm or a schism in consciousness. . . ." She is echoing something she had said earlier about her mother, "*If* one could stay near her always, there would be no break in consciousness. . . ." It is striking, I think, that she does not complain of her mother's coldness, but of the many people who "come and interrupt" their relationship.

In short, H. D. has shown, in the transference, how her mystical and religious wishes hark back to the early mother-child relationship. The timeless world of myth becomes, for her, a way of avoiding gaps, breaks, interruptions. In earliest infancy, the child does not perceive itself as a being separate from its mother. Only as it must wait, expect, trust in that nurturing other to come and minister to its needs does it begin to recognize that that other is a separate being; that therefore it is itself a separate being. In other words, our very sense of identity is predicated upon our ability to trust in a nurturing other. If too much hate and frustration are mobilized by that other (as in "interruptions"), that sense of "basic trust" and with it, identity, will be impaired. In later life, [Erik] Erikson has shown, political ideologies, personal love, or religious faith can serve the maternal function, gratifying "the simple and fervent wish for a hallucinatory sense of unity with a maternal matrix."

Thus Freud interpreted H. D.'s mystical vision on Corfu "as a desire for union with [your] mother." In the transference, he becomes that mother: "'Why did you think you had to tell me? . . . But you felt you wanted to tell your mother.'" Indeed, H. D.'s whole faith in Freud and psychoanalysis should be so interpreted: "The Professor had said in the very beginning that I had come to Vienna hoping to find my mother."

It is not surprising, then, that H. D. uses images of fluids to describe the psychoanalytic process. She had entered analysis because she felt she was, like other intellectuals, "drifting," that she was "a narrow birchbark canoe" being swept into the "cataract" of war. Her friends provided only "a deluge of brilliant talk," but no "safe harbour." Thus she sees herself as "a shipwrecked child" turning to old Captain January. "The flow of associated images," the "fountainhead of highest truth," "the current [that] ran too deep"—H. D.'s images of fluids suggest, beautifully, the way something which is experienced passively, as an overpowering and terrifying deluge or flood, can, in the microcosm of the analytic relationship, be accepted and mastered. "He would stand guardian, he would turn the whole stream of consciousness back into useful, into *irrigation* channels. . . ."

Other images of fluids show the feeling of "oceanic" unity that is related

to that first unity with the mother. Freud she identifies as naming and discovering "a great stream or ocean underground" that, "overflowing," produces inspiration, madness, or creative idea. This ocean transcends all
barriers of time and space. Thus, for any patient, "his particular stream, his
personal life, could run clear of obstruction into the great river of humanity,
hence to the sea of superhuman perfection . . ." (and again the issue of gender
colors H. D.'s visions of immortality and fusion). H. D. had indeed "come
to Vienna hoping to find [her] mother," even as she had found her on Corfu.

She began to see pictures outlined in light on the wall of her hotel room.
The first was a head-and-shoulders silhouette of a soldier or airman with a
visored cap. The second "was the conventional outline of a goblet or cup,
actually suggesting the mystic chalice, but it was the familiar goblet shape
we all know, with round base and glass-stem." The third is another mythological adaptation of a familiar object: the stand for a small spirit-lamp
metamorphosed into the tripod on which the prophetess at Delphi sat. H. D.
sees the tripod as the triad of religion, art, and medicine. These figures—
hieroglyphs, she calls them—appear like "formal patterns" stamped on playing cards, but it is very much part of H. D.'s psychic patterns that she cannot
tell whether she is projecting the images or whether "they are projected from
outside."

Around the base of the tripod appears a swarm of tiny people, like
insects. "They were people, they were annoying—I did not hate people, I
did not especially resent any one person." H. D. seems to accept Freud's
interpretation of the vision "as a suppressed desire for forbidden 'signs and
wonders,' breaking bounds, a suppressed desire to be a Prophetess, to be
important anyway, megalomania they call it . . . ," and perhaps this megalomanic fantasy is why the people appear as a swarm of "small midges." At
any rate, the people disappear, and the pictures begin to move upward.

Two dots of light appear and trace lines toward each other until they
meet and become one line. She is stiff, says H. D., as though she were looking
at the Gorgon head. The dots form another line, then another, then a series.
H. D. feels as though she is drowning: "I must be born again or break
utterly." The lines become a Jacob's ladder linking heaven and earth.

The last figure forms: "There she is, I call her she; I call her Niké,
Victory," around her a pattern of half-*S*'s—question marks. "She is a com-
mon-or-garden angel . . . ," three-dimensional, floating up the ladder, "free
and with wings." "Niké, Victory seemed to be the clue, seemed to be my
own especial sign or part of my hieroglyph." "I thought, 'Helios, the sun . . .'
And I shut off, 'cut out' before the final picture, before (you might say) the
explosion took place." H. D. let go, then, from complete exhaustion, but

[her friend] Bryher [Winifred Ellerman] saw "the last concluding symbol." "She said, it was a circle like the sun-disc and a figure within the disc; a man, she thought, was reaching out to draw the image of a woman (my Niké?) into the sun beside him."

Obviously this vision has an almost unbelievable richness of symbol, association, and theme. It consolidates a whole mass of charged materials for H. D. No wonder she felt completely exhausted; no wonder Freud singled out this vision "as the most dangerous or the only actually dangerous 'symptom'. . . ." Indeed, she originally entitled the memoir "Writing on the Wall," but went along with Norman Holmes Pearson's suggestion of a change.

As one would expect, the final vision is the least defended against or disguised, the first vision the most so. To the last picture, H. D. associated memories of her father and mother. Clearly, then, the most obvious interpretation of the man in the sun-disc is her Apollo-father, and to be the chosen woman of the father would indeed involve an "explosion." H. D. herself, however, suggests another interpretation and association: ". . . The shrine of Helios (Hellas, Helen) had been really the main objective of my journey." "I was physically in Greece, in Hellas (Helen). I had come home to the glory that was Greece," and she identifies the phrase as from "Edgar Allan Poe's much-quoted *Helen,* and my mother's name was Helen."

Such associations take us back to early, oral wishes for a timeless at-oneness with the mother; now H. D. is victorious in her quest. There is, however, still another pattern of fusion: the vision is not only H. D.'s; it is also Bryher's, a further blurring of the boundaries between self and nurturing other. Dots come together to form a Jacob's ladder linking heaven to earth: the dots themselves merge; the ladder from earth to the realm of the gods suggests a child's wish to merge into the world of the parents.

To this part of the vision, however, H. D. associates staring at the Gorgon's head. There are few universal symbols in psychoanalysis, and Freud was quite right to caution H. D. against one-to-one symbolic decodings. But Medusa's head is a virtual universal: it represents the child's trauma at the sight of the female genitals accompanied by the horrifying fear that castration is indeed performed. Here H. D. identifies herself with Perseus, guided by "Athené (or was it Hermes, Mercury?)," and the Gorgon head is not only "an enemy to be dealt with," "the ugly Head or Source of evil," but also "He was himself to manipulate his weapon, this ugly severed head of the enemy of Wisdom and Beauty. . . ." She seems to be saying the vision—the sight itself—is the combination of male weapon and ugly, female hostility. In one of her poems she describes lovemaking as two weapons one of which will "break" the other.

Still working backwards through H. D.'s images, we come to the tripod, a homely, familiar object. It is the "base" for the spirit-lamp, but it is also what the Pythoness of Delphi sat on. It may also represent what H. D. sat on; certainly her description of it stresses the emptiness of its circles. Yet it is this stand that is associated with her megalomania—again, we seem to be coming to the theme of overcompensating for what she feels is the inferior quality of her feminine body. What the prophetess sits on is at once "homely" and "all the more an object to be venerated."

The "soldier or airman" H. D. identifies as "dead brother? lost friend?" In any case, he seems to represent that hard, weaponed masculinity that H. D. longed for. Between this masculine figure and the tripod is the chalice, another "familiar" object transformed. H. D. associates it with the "mystic chalice," hence with a quest of some kind. Like the tripod, it is empty, and its place in the sequence suggests a relation between oral needs and the quest for a lost masculinity or masculine figure.

To sum up, in the mystical vision H. D. does two things: she concretizes the abstract; she mythologizes the commonplace. The vision on Corfu brings us to the heart of the H. D. myth. It was implicit in her first meeting with Freud: to approach the outer object of an inner desire through an intermediary. We can now explicate those terms. The intermediary is perfect, timeless, symbolic (that is, mythological, hieroglyphic), combining past and future, male and female, with "no interruptions." The outer object tends to be hard, real, everyday, prosaic, even brutal; the inner desire, vague, soft, empty, abstract, and spiritual. We can make at least a preliminary statement of the H. D. myth: *when I concretize the spiritual or mythologize the everyday, I create a perfect, timeless hieroglyph-world which I can be and be in.* Or, very briefly, *I want to close the gap with signs. . . .*

It would be easy to see H. D.'s longing to create, to fuse with hard objects as purely defensive or pathological: the attempt to recreate a lost masculinity or a "hard," ungiving mother. But it is perfectly clear that this symptom or character-trait had adaptive virtues as well. To it, we owe H. D.'s interest in and ability to bring out her unconscious life in enduring artistic forms.

> But we fight for life,
> we fight, they say, for breath,
>
> so what good are your scribblings?
> this—we take them with us

> beyond death; Mercury, Hermes, Thoth
> invented the script, letters, palette;
>
> the indicated flute or lyre-notes
> on papyrus or parchment
>
> are magic, indelibly stamped
> on the atmosphere somewhere,
>
> forever; remember, O Sword,
> you are the younger brother, the latter-born
>
> your Triumph, however exultant,
> must one day be over,
>
> *in the beginning*
> *was the Word.*
>   (*The Walls Do Not Fall*)

In her Corfu vision, she paused between images "as if a painter had stepped back from a canvas the better to regard the composition of the picture, or a musician had paused at the music-stand. . . ." ". . . This writing-on-the-wall is merely an extension of the artist's mind, a *picture* or an illustrated poem. . . ." ". . . Dreams are as varied as are the books we read, the pictures we look at or the people we meet." "The books and the people merge in this world of fantasy and imagination. . . ."

To create a work of art was to immortalize an inner wish, to create, as well, an immortal person ministering to an immortal self.

> grape, knife, cup, wheat
>
> are symbols in eternity,
> and every concrete object
>
> has abstract value, is timeless
> in the dream parallel
>
> whose relative sigil has not changed
> since Nineveh and Babel.
>   (*The Walls Do Not Fall*)

Sigil, signet, *signum*—she talks about these words in *Tribute to Freud*. "And as I write that last word, there flashes into my mind the associated *in hoc signum* or rather, it must be *in hoc signo* and *vinces*." We are reminded of the "megalomania" Freud found in the "dangerous symptom" of the Corfu vision. "Signet," too, has its associations, among them "the royal signature, usually only the initials of the sovereign's name. (I have used my initials H. D. consistently as my writing signet or sign-manual, though it is only, at this very moment . . . that I realize that my writing signature has anything remotely suggesting sovereignty or the royal manner.)"

I feel sadness for a woman who had to become a royal and mythic sign to make up for all those missing things. But I honor the poet. She did indeed close up the gap with signs and, in doing so, left to us a body of poems for which we can be grateful.

She also left behind this unique document, *Tribute to Freud,* from which we have been able to infer the H. D. myth as it evolved through the successive psychosexual stages of her own development and as it revealed itself through Freud's taking on a succession of roles in the transference: brother, father, oedipal mother, and, most important, the cosmic, oral mother of earliest infancy. To repeat, the H. D. myth, as expressed in the memoir, involves an attempt *to close up the gap between inner and outer, spiritual and physical, male and female, by perfect, timeless signs which she can be and be in.* Such a myth is not just an abstraction but develops in stages dynamically, toward an adult life-style that permeates "all [she] did and thought."

As for so many lyric poets, the psychosexual mode that dominates H. D.'s psyche is the earliest: the oral. At her very center, H. D. wishes and fears to fuse with, be devoured by, close the gap between herself and—her mother, felt as a timeless, uninterrupted, unbroken mystical level of experience. The wish (and fear) develops in two directions: she transforms the imperfections and frustrations of the real world into more perfect poetic signs; she concretizes inchoate, inner longing into hard, tangible, reachable realities—again, usually mythological. In classical myth and other poetic signs, H. D. found the compromise: perfections she could have. She becomes the poet of hard, cold things or, alternatively, bristly pine trees and hedge-hogs. The strategy is a cosmic one and gives rise to imagery of oceans, floods, her sustaining use of mythology and her destructive fantasies of fiery world-destruction.

The first, oral, psychosexual stage colors its successors: anal, phallic, oedipal. H. D.'s writings have very little of the anal mode in them. What there is seems focused on the transformation of soft, dirty, oily, or raglike objects into hard, firm works of art. Soft materials might be forced out of her by another, might belong to that other (a version of the earlier fusion), while hard objects are her own creation. The phallic mode has more importance: H. D.'s wish to create a hard, phallic object so as to replace a lost masculinity. To yield in a feminine way is to melt, dissolve, flow away, or be transformed. It is at this phallic level that she wishes instead to fuse with the winged and weaponed Mercuries—ultimately, her brother (and, back of him, father, then mother). The oedipal level of H. D.'s development seems to have the usual triangles, but primitivized by her pervasive oral fantasies. Thus she sees both mother- and father-figures as mythically or religiously or magically powerful. The usual wish to *have* the father becomes, for her, a wish to *be* her father with all his phallic potency and castrating power. Behind this oedipal wish is the oral one: if she can fuse with brother or father, she can have and be mother—still conceived as the cosmic supplier the infant longs for.

Such developmental phases one can identify in any human being. When we see them in a creative writer, though, our curiosity is piqued. We tend to ask, as the Cardinal asks of Ariosto, "Where did you find so many stories, Lodovico?" It is not too difficult to see the connections between H. D.'s developmental stages and such literary insights as Professor [Joseph N.] Riddel's:

> The threatened flower of self, caught between the great maternal ocean and the hard, firm, enduring shore (the fragile flower and the stalwart tree) compose the essential landmarks of H. D.'s condition. They are the components of her recurrent myth—her *cogito*—in its purest form.

> Inwardness is projected as transient and insubstantial—soft and decaying like a fragile flower . . . or as the decaying fragments of a heat-oppressed space.

> The poet affirms her identity not by solving the mystery but by reifying it.

But how can one locate in the stages of H. D.'s development the wellsprings of her creativity? What, for example, is the relation between her creative writing and her mental health or illness?

To close the gap with signs. H. D.'s myth could have taken a psychotic or pre-psychotic form. Apparently it did, if we credit Freud's singling out of "megalomania" in the Corfu vision. The terrible losses of the 1914–1919 period fitted into the pattern of her childhood deprivation; psychotic mechanisms were mobilized to "close the gap." As for neurosis, H. D. makes it clear that part of her wish to close the gap took neurotic forms—anxieties about her body: penis envy, her height, her femininity. Whether there was character disorder—perversion, sociopathy, schizoid tendencies—her silence about her adult life makes it impossible to say. If, however, we apply Freud's basic criteria of normal functioning—*lieben und arbeiten;* to love and to work—it is clear that H. D. was a productive poet and a sufficient mother. She was functioning in large part as a healthy adult.

In short, H. D.'s account of her analysis with Freud makes it clear that creativity does not stem from mental illness; neither is it a simple alternative. Rather, the key variable is *style*. Both illness ("megalomania," to take the gravest case) and creative activity (imagistically rendered myths) will have the same style. Put another way, both will act out the same underlying myth. The megalomanic vision will distort reality, the Imagist mythographer will create an artifact, both "to close the gap with signs."

"Where did you find so many stories, Lodovico?" What turned H. D. to poetry? The strong forces in H. D.'s myth must have happened to many women: a style of mothering that created "gaps," the distant father, the envied brothers. But not every woman who experienced such a childhood became a poet. What was critical in H. D.'s life? In other words, plenty of children experienced the "gaps"; what made H. D. take "signs" as a way of dealing with "gaps"? She was born in Bethlehem, Pennsylvania. She lived on Church Street. At any early age, she experienced the special rituals and language of her mother's religion, the Moravian Brotherhood. Her brothers used words she could not understand. Her father would look at stars, numbers, hieroglyphs, but not at her. One gets, I think, a feel for, glimmerings of, the factors in H. D.'s early environment that made "signs" (religious, alphabetic, hieroglyphic, numerical, mythic) the most economical way to close the gap.

Only a full biography could make firm connections, but a preliminary formulation seems to emerge. Healthy infancy involves a series of needs, longings, fears, and frustrations. Those in the early mother-child relation seem to have most to do with literary creativity. However, these earliest stresses are much the same for most people. They vary but not enough to say why one person becomes a writer and another not. Highly variable, however, are the possibilities the environment offers for dealing with these "gaps." (And, of course, heredity also imposes limitations on these possibilities.)

> Under the name of "the principle of multiple function" [Robert] Waelder has described a phenomenon of cardinal importance in ego psychology. This principle expresses the tendency of the organism toward inertia, that is, the tendency to achieve a maximum of effect with a minimum of effort. Among various possible actions that one is chosen which best lends itself to the simulta-

neous satisfaction of demands from several sources. An action
fulfilling a demand of the external world may at the same time
result in instinctual gratification and in satisfying the superego.
The mode of reconciling various tasks to one another is characteristic for a given personality. Thus the ego's habitual modes of
adjustment to the external world, the id, and the superego, and
the characteristic types of combining these modes with one another, constitute character.

(Otto Fenichel, *The Psychoanalytic Theory of Neurosis*)

"Signs" evidently achieved for H. D. a maximum of effect with a minimum
of effort and hence became part of both her character and her poetry, her
life-style and her literary style, or, in Yeats's term, her myth. In another
environment, storytelling, role-playing, verbal games like rhyme, or coined
languages—any of these might have proved more economical and so made
for a different kind of writer. Creative writing, like any other act "in character," satisfies a combination of pleasure-giving and defensive needs.

What is striking, though, is that these determinants toward writing and
toward a certain style of writing are not buried in the obscurity of infancy
(at least not for H. D.). They are there for the biographer to see—provided
he knows what to look for. H. D., by revealing herself in the memoir of
Freud, enables us to formulate an H. D. myth. (For other writers, one would
hypothesize such a myth from the writings alone—as Yeats did for Shakespeare. But H. D.'s work with Freud gives her "myth" a special validity.)
Once formulated, the myth tells us which of the external biographical factors
would be likely to combine with her inner needs to give rise to H. D.'s special
poetic character.

In short, H. D.'s generous revelation of herself in *Tribute to Freud* gives
us more than insight into H. D. It leads to a general method of psychobiog-
raphy that, without her, we would not have. We can be grateful to her not
only for her poems, but for her willingness to lend us the insights she achieved
with the "blameless physician." Every biographer must be in her debt, and
Tribute to Freud is a Tribute to H. D. as well.

A. KINGSLEY WEATHERHEAD

Style in H. D.'s Novels

Contemporary assumptions about style are that it is not a special garment assumed but an outgrowth of personality and experience, with features not consciously chosen. A pronouncement of Sir Walter Raleigh's about style, though not very recent, is in tune with our current expressionistic concepts: "Write, and after you have attained to some control over the instrument, you write yourself down whether you will or no. There is no vice, however unconscious, no virtue, however shy, no touch of meanness or of generosity in your character, that will not pass on to the paper." So also, one would assume, with experience: not necessarily for trivial practitioners but surely for writers involved in their craft, "whatever Miss T. eats / Turns into Miss T." and is discernible.

A sentiment such as the following [by H. P. Collins in *Modern Poetry*], therefore, seems dated: "one imagines that H. D. had a mysterious (and most enviable!) faculty of keeping the transiencies of modern life and the spirit of poetry in different compartments of the mind. A flight from life, the humanist might be expected to object of H. D.'s lyrics." There is a character in *Palimpsest*, H. D.'s first novel, who remarks, "People were always kind about her poetry not understanding, saying she was cold—cold—cold. . . ." Douglas Bush [in *Mythology and the Romantic Tradition in English Poetry*] calls her a poet of escape; and the charge elsewhere is that she runs away from the demands of life. But which demands, one may enquire, can in fact be

From *Contemporary Literature* 10, no. 4 (Autumn 1969). © 1969 by the Board of Regents of the University of Wisconsin System.

run away from? It is only loose talk, of course. Her writing is not a simple escape from real life; inasmuch as it may be a means of entering more deeply into experience, exploring it more profoundly in the form of an artifact, it may be a means of mitigating and exorcising grief, but not merely escaping. Indeed, in studying her prose one would rather wonder how H. D. could bear to probe so repeatedly, if variously, into her own bitter experiences. Her poetry dwells on them too, but more indirectly: she lost her first baby in 1915 "from shock and repercussions of war news broken . . . in a rather brutal fashion" [*Tribute to Freud*], and she then proceeded to translate Euripides' *Iphigeneia*. And, the high noon of the New Criticism being past, it is safe to relate with decent tenuousness the biographical detail to the literary activity: H. D. was not in the ordinary sense escaping anything.

Similarly one may ask of the poems in *Hymen* (1921) whether they are an escape or whether they are not rather the fingering of wounds inflicted by some of the painful experiences of 1919, in which year, having lost her husband, Richard Aldington, to another woman, H. D. received news of the death of her father following the death of her brother in action in France and came herself near to dying from double pneumonia on the eve of giving birth to a daughter. There is the poem "Demeter," for instance, in which this hard, big-limbed goddess compares herself with the soft, alluring Aphrodite and asks,

> am I a spouse, his or any,
> am I a woman, or goddess or queen,
> to be met by a god with a smile—and left?
>   ("Demeter")

In "She Contrasts with Herself Hippolyta," H. D. tries to scrutinize the situation of this untamed amazon when betrayed into giving birth:

> What did she think
> when all her strength
> was twisted for his bearing.

Biographical criticism admits of no certainty. But it is a reasonably safe proposition that H. D. was fully committed to her work and escaped nothing of her experience.

The subject of injured women, most frequently deserted women, is a regularly repeated feature of all H. D.'s writing. Her own losses are reflected more directly in the novels than in the poems; one novel presents not only the heroine in her familiar grief but also her effort to deal with it by poetry.

"Murex," the second part of *Palimpsest,* is concerned among other things to show how the wounding experience can become poetry; Omar Khayyam is repeatedly quoted to the effect that "nowhere blows so red the rose as where some buried Caesar bled." The murex, the shell-fish which provides the purple dye and which Browning made famous in a cryptic poem, is the poetic power that can render experience into poetry; it is not just a skill or a technique but a disposition of mind of self-effacement and even love.

H. D. acts out her own tribulations in her writing, but the writing is nevertheless highly stylized; in the poems, the "news" is refined almost away and the form dominates, with the result that to various critics her poetry has seemed empty or at least thin. There is more matter in the novels: most of the figures of suffering women, central to all of them, are more particularly related to the authoress than are the figures in the poems. The figure of Julia Ashton in the *roman à clef, Bid Me to Live (A Madrigal),* is especially close to H. D. herself and undergoes H. D.'s own personal experiences. Although they have more news in them than the poetry and more unrefracted personal characteristics and experience, the novels are still quite markedly stylized artifacts.

H. D. is of course writing out of a literary atmosphere created in London ten or fifteen years earlier by people of her own acquaintance, of which Wyndham Lewis remarks [in *Blasting and Bombardiering*] that it "resulted in [T. E.] Hulme and myself preferring something anti-naturalist and 'abstract' to Nineteenth Century naturalism, in pictures and in statues. . . . Man was not the hero of our universe." Rather than follow general convention into the creation of realistic persons in realistic events, H. D. seems to use the feelings and behavior of people to form designs, by symmetry and asymmetry, counterpoint, juxtaposition, repetition, and—what is a somewhat special kind of repetition in her style—superimposition. The end proposed is a pattern of sorts: the experience we are to settle for as readers is not merely the discovery of what happens to the figures who compose it. Even the relatively realistic novel, *Bid Me to Live,* bears the subtitle "A Madrigal," which presumably claims for it the elaborate stylization of this art form rather than verisimilitude. All this is to mark a leaning rather than to say that the reader makes no human but only aesthetic responses to the novels. H. D. perhaps wanted to emulate the Greeks in the best part of the classic period when, in her own words, "the archaic abstraction became humanized but not yet over-humanized" (*Tribute to Freud*).

Palimpsest (1926) consists of three parts, each a long short story showing many affinities with the others in theme, plot, and detail. The first part is called "Hipparchia" and presents this Greek woman (anachronistically the

daughter of Crates the Cynic, c. 320 B.C.) as the mistress of Marius, a Roman
officer, at some time ("circa 75 B.C.," according to the title) subsequent to
Rome's conquest of Corinth. Hipparchia leaves Marius by mutual consent,
their union being ultimately unsatisfactory to both. She goes to Capua with
Verrus, another Roman. But she questions now whether she loves Verrus,
and in the fact of the questioning she recognizes that she does not. Returning
to Rome, she meets Marius, who had written her passionate letters from the
battlefield; they are again unable, however, to engage each other. Hipparchia
leaves for Tusculum, where she proceeds with the writing she and her foster
brother had been at work on before he had been shot by Roman troops. It
is a book of scientific exposition with poems, translations from the Greek,
inset; and she intends that ultimately this rehabilitation of the Greek will
destroy Rome. She develops Roman fever; and into her delirium, in which
Osiris had come to claim her, enters a young woman, Julia, who has admired
and learned Hipparchia's poetry by heart. Julia, with her father, is engaged
upon a history of the Macedonian conquest; and she has now come to invite
Hipparchia to accompany them on a journey to Alexandria. Hipparchia
agrees to go.

Part 2, "Murex," is set in "War and post-war London (circa 1916–
1926 A.D.)." The heroine, Raymonde Ransome, is also a poet; she writes
under the pseudonym Ray Bart. She is called upon to listen to the complaint
of a young woman, Ermentrude, whose lover has been appropriated by another, a woman called Mavis, who ten years earlier (1916) had seduced
Raymonde's own husband, Freddie, Raymonde having been in the hospital
at the time giving birth to a dead child. It is these experiences she is engaged
in transmuting into poetry, as Raymonde metamorphoses into Ray Bart.

Part 3, "Secret Name," covers a day or two of the Egyptian experiences
of Mrs. Helen Fairwood, secretary to an Egyptologist. She meets an ex-army
captain, Rafton, who takes her on a moonlight expedition to the Karnak
ruins. After it is over she establishes in her mind that the moonlit excursion
was only an excursion and that Rafton was only an ordinary ex-captain.
(She is not about to be conquered by this Romanesque officer, as Greece was
conquered by Rome.) The section concludes with Helen acting as chaperone
and confidant to a younger woman who has successfully become engaged to
be married during the same expedition.

In each part a woman who has been deserted or has declined a sexual
relationship alleviates her own distress by identifying herself with the cares
or concerns of a younger woman, or by coming under the wing of the latter,
as H. D. had in fact come under that of Bryher, who redeemed her from
sickness in 1919 and took her abroad. The mere outlines of the stories,

however, give very little sense of the nature of this novel; for beneath the
plots thus baldly summarized the novel is dense with minor details and
motifs, mutually illuminating or justifying each other and linking together
the parts of the whole—such small and otherwise inert particulars as the
weight of his armor on Marius pressing him down and the weight of fleeces
oppressing Hipparchia, Hipparchia's nourishment when sick and Raymonde's inability to get supper for herself, and scores of other such cross
references. There is so much of this, in fact, that one's major impression of
each part and of the novel as a whole is that it is a tissue of sensations lightly
matching one another, woven together by mysterious thin threads of plot
and theme.

The prose has a variety of calculated auditory effects. The opening pages
present a dialogue, in flashback, between Marius and Hipparchia, a dialogue,
we understand, that they have often held, conducted now in the stately
rhythm of the sarabande. Words and phrases are carefully selected not for
sense alone but for the ear—for rhymes, half-rhymes, and cadence—as in the
following preciously built passage: "He hated her yet waited on her entrance,
himself somewhat servile, heavy, serf-like, weary, as suddenly in a moment
he was flooded with a realisation of his peculiar longing." In the dialogue
occur a number of phrases and sentences that are to be repeated throughout
this part of the novel: "Greece was now lost, the cities disassociated from
any central ruling"; "Romans are wine pressers"; and others, including the
line from a poem by Antipater of Sidon, the whole of which is reproduced
in translation: "Where Corinth, charm incarnate, are your shrines?"—the
question Hipparchia will in the end answer, "Greece is a spirit."

The prose of "Hipparchia" recalls Walter Pater, whom H. D. mentions
as one figure in her early reading; that of "Murex" is entirely stream of
consciousness, recalling Joyce; and that of "Secret Name" largely the same,
though the stream does not flow quite so fast. Not only in "Hipparchia"
but in the other parts, too, the prose contains words and phrases that are
regularly repeated, which punctuate the monologue with the meanings that
they had in their first usages, now brought forth momentarily in the new
context. In some cases, though, by the mere fact of repetition the meanings
tend to be deadened, and we respond more primitively, registering the sound
alone as if a part of a ritual. In "Murex" Raymonde's memory of 1916 is
dominated by war, in particular by marching feet. Thus whenever the 1916
memories invade the present she hears the feet marching to Victoria Station.
"If Mavis wanted the young man and if Mavis got the young man—All's fair
in love and—feet, feet, feet, feet. They had all forgotten." Throughout Raymonde's internal monologue the words "feet-feet-feet-feet" continually recur.

They are a synecdoche for the War, and behind that for war, and behind that for the endless cycle of birth and death; but in the end they come to be registered not so much by the interpreting mind as simply by the receiving ear, like a repeated phrase or melodic line in music, slowing the movement; so too with another repeated phrase in the same part of the novel, "her panache, her not quite diminished glory," responded to at first intellectually but later merely with the ear.

When the flow of thought becomes hectic, associations of sounds and ideas as well as repetitions run rife:

> *Who fished the murex up?* And where? Not here, not here, Freddie. Drift and obliteration and Mavis in her green-blue and aquamarines. Who—fished—the—murex—up? It must be late, late. Time for bed. Pull down the wine-blue cover and unroll one's night things and sleep—sleep—sleep—bed—Ermy. One couldn't betray one of her race for nothing. And thou too, Brutus. Where some buried Caesar bled. Bled—bed. Ermy on a bed. She could see her. Bed, bled, dead.
>
> ("Murex," *Palimpsest*)

The rhymes carry the thought forward by association of sound. The fact that words rhyme is not necessarily fortuitous, but may be a signal from the subconscious mind. Long before her Freudian analysis H. D. was aware of the long-range reverberating powers of individual words, the meanings behind puns, alliteration, rhymes, and such apparent verbal play.

But in this passage and in many others like it, H. D.'s policy is to bring items into contact with their precedents in the past—a practice reflecting *in parvo* what is done in the novel on a larger scale, as the title suggests. "Palimpsest" is defined in the epigraph as "a parchment from which one writing has been erased to make room for another"; we are presumably intended to remark the superimpositions—at one end of the scale, of images, and at the other, of large situations. "Art," Raymonde Ransome muses, "wasn't seen any more in one plane, in one perspective, in one dimension. One didn't any more see things like that. Impressions were reflected now ... they were overlaid like old photographic negatives one on top of another." Thus behind Ermy's betrayal was Raymonde's own; behind this, Caesar's; out of Caesar's, the rose; out of Ermy's, the poem. It is an instance, however minor, of the principle that constitutes a major feature of H. D.'s style in this novel and its successors: the past, antiquity or recent, is superimposed upon the present, giving meaning and deriving life; images are superimposed upon images, meanings upon experience, characters upon other characters or upon their alter egos, one part of a novel upon another, and gods upon men.

Her style reflects her way of viewing experience. What she says of Freud might be said of herself, if she means that he made the past live: "It was not that he conjured up the past and invoked the future. It was a present that was in the past or a past that was in the future" (*Tribute to Freud*). Her style is informed by a vision of experience colored by her own private typology, according to which she sees Freud, for example, as a latter-day Hercules, the man who preceded her to his couch as Mercury, and the lens, the paper-knife, and the paperweight on her father's desk as sacred objects. Such a way of seeing is not simply an outcome of her psychoanalysis in the thirties; years before she met Freud she habitually viewed her fictional characters as superimposed upon one another or upon figures of the past, and in this manner she often brings the departed to her presence or the dead to life in the form of one avatar or other.

This whole tendency of style, however, represents only one way of seeing life. There is an alternative way that gives rise to an opposing tendency: it does not look back less frequently, but it also resorts to the past not to bring it forward alive into the present but in order to find in it some retreat from the flux and anarchy of immediate contemporary experience. It looks back in the hope of finding the immutable or the stiff Platonic form; or very often, when not looking back, it reduces what it sees to dead geometrical shapes and ordered patterns, impairing life in order to see it steadily; or it insists on seeing movement as a series of tableaux, and soft, protean things as perdurable and fixed. These two attitudes to life and the two tendencies of style to which they give rise are not mutually exclusive; on the contrary, H. D. may swing rapidly from one manner of seeing experience to the other.

The attitudes to experience, the discussion of them, and the respective adoption and rejection of one or the other provide a large part of the subject-matter for H. D.'s novels. One may say, these are *about* style to a greater or lesser extent: it is the business of the heroines to discover how they should view their experience and, in most cases, how they should translate it into literature. The question comes to the forefront by stages throughout the years of H. D.'s novel-writing career: in *Bid Me to Live*, finally, a view of life as static and encompassable in familiar geometric patterns is replaced by one that opens up a new dimension and identifies characters and situations with their precedents, bringing these to life; what is called the "stylized classic manner" is roundly rejected, and the heroine develops a style from which she has withdrawn herself in a wise passiveness so that her subjects can live.

The terms of vision and style are not immediately apparent as such in the earlier novels; but the terms these do use are parallel and share some of the same implications. In the last part of *Palimpsest* the alternative modes of vision are the definite and the indefinite, respectively, the clear outline and the blur, the measurable and the immeasurable; and these are associated with Athens and Egypt. Some of these alternatives may be seen in the following thought of Helen Fairwood in "Secret Name," who is thinking first about Egypt:

> Here there was no need of measure, of self-scale, of flinging (as at Paestum, as at Athens) oneself upward, stretched tip-toe to one's highest spiritual height, measuring oneself by the measure, so strictly subtle, of the gods. The Athenian made a god, strict and subtle against which a human soul could (by standing tip-toe) by making the greatest of physical and psychic effort, yet contrast himself. He was (to the god) a brother, dwarfed yet still a human relative. In Egypt there was this unassuming comfort. One measured oneself by new and as yet unpremeditated standards. Crouched on the temple wall, she was some long and tenuous insect, drawn inward to the heart of a moon-flower.
>
> ("Secret Name," *Palimpsest*)

Again, in other parts of the novel, the terms are not identical with these, and the issues are less clear; it is as if "Secret Name" were a kaleidoscope through which we see the disorganized glittering fragments of "Hipparchia" and "Murex" reflected in a pattern. In the first part Hipparchia considers two opposing ways of seeing experience: "Could actual memory," she wonders, "be exceeded by mere imagining? Could vision supersede sheer natural contour of flower petal?" Toward the end of the first part she identifies Verrus with Osiris and refers to him as an anodyne, just as Egypt is an anodyne to Helen. His replacement of Marius, who is associated with endeavor, looks forward to the passiveness which, in *Bid Me to Live,* is finally decreed an integral part of style. In "Murex" Raymonde, luxuriating in the "drift and drug of obliteration" of London, becomes Ray Bart, the intellectual poet, and plans to leave for Cret-d'y-Vau and the "ice and shale and snow and inspiration." She feels about this place as Helen feels about Athens: it "seemed to raise its white marble, a challenge"; earlier she is aware of its "disproportionate background of magnificence," and she feels she would be "dwarfed in Cret-d'y-Vau . . . only the jagged points of that hateful and domineering mountain to drag her mind up, up, up to its highest attainment."

The two cultures of Athens and Egypt attract different parts of the personality of Helen Fairwood or, as the novel expresses it, her separate selves. Other heroines too in this and the other novels are presented each as owning two or more separate selves, one self sometimes revealing male characteristics—the self of Hipparchia that is identified with her antifeminist mother, Raymonde as Ray Bart, Helen in boyish shirt open at the throat. The women move from one self to another, and the move is often associated with one from a cold setting to a warm one or the reverse: Hipparchia for instance, warm as the servant of Aphrodite, is cold as the servant of Athene. She leaves Marius, who is characteristically associated with the ruby and dull amber brazier lighted in the bedroom, to live with Verrus, who is associated with the cold and with the repeated assertion, "Braziers burning in a bedroom stifle breathing." In "Murex," one enjoys "drift and drug of obliteration" in London in a warm autumnal season, which Raymonde deliberately exchanges for the cold of Cret-d'y-Vau. In the last part of the novel the heroine in her cold bed reverts from the "anodine of Egypt" to Greek intellection, restoring the earlier mystical experiences in the ruins of Karnak to their proper human perspective, relegating the soldier Rafton, who in the moonlight had seemed an avatar with a secret name, to become "the most ordinary of ex-army captains." Later with a cool wind from the desert, modernity sweeps over the scene that had previously lent itself to mystery.

The heroines themselves undergo sudden descents from mysteriousness to the light of common day: Hipparchia, one moment "stark, intense, honey-coloured, fragrant" and the next "simply a weary mistress, seated, yawning"; Helen Fairwood, like "any nursemaid dallying in any garrison town." Although we see her finally in an Athens mood, Helen has earlier recognized the need of balance between the two worlds,

> fearful from the start, lest for very rapture of this other world, this anodine of Egypt, she might loose her slightly more familiar, hard-won, specific Attic paradise. Aware too of danger in another direction. She might so very easily, with so slight a mental faux-pas, through curiosity, mere inquisitiveness, desire to use the steel she had so hardly won, forego, past remedy, her right of entry to this just-found Egypt. On the specific prowl. She feared lest with cautious Attic brain, she might freeze at a moment of discovery. Lest at a moment where cool pulse is requisite, she might flame into some self-destructive aura.
>
> ("Secret Name," *Palimpsest*)

Balance apparently is to be kept; one is to respect Attic measurement, but one is to remain open to vague Asiatic immensities. Hipparchia, too, at the end of the first part of the novel appears to be balancing two worlds, when, not to avoid Greek values but because Greece is not lost, she agrees to go to Alexandria with the new-found friend: " 'Greece is a spirit. Someone said *Greece is a spirit. Greece is not lost.* I will come with you.' " One cannot pin too much on the incident—an incident accounted for, in part anyway, by its closeness to the experience H. D. had herself lived through in 1919 when Bryher promised her on her sickbed to take her abroad (in fact, to Greece). But the same sense that one set of values and associations will complement the other is derived also from H. D.'s next novel, *Hedylus*.

The novel is set in the island of Samos where Hedylus the poet and his mother, the courtesan Hedyle, with whom the novel is principally concerned, came to live ten years earlier, having stopped there on their way from Athens to Alexandria. Hedylus has been invited to go to Alexandria, but his mother is anxious that the boy not go. Meanwhile Hedylus, declaiming his own poetry at a virtually inaccessible point of the beach, is interrupted by a stranger, whom he intermittently takes to be a god, who leads him back to the guest house where he is quartered and invites Hedylus to accompany him to India. Hedylus, however, goes at length to Alexandria, while the stranger visits Hedyle and proves to be Demion, her ex-lover. These and many other details are transmitted in stately, decorated prose.

The Athens-Egypt dialectic is again present in this novel; and although there is little enough to reinforce them, the connotations these place names gained in *Palimpsest* are again more or less appropriate. Hedylus is of Athens, but not, in the beginning, Athenian; Athenian to him is "what we would and can't be," something he must achieve and, we understand, something he does achieve by embarking for Egypt, inasmuch as the last word of the novel designates him Athenian. At the same time Hedylus, who identifies his mother with Athens, recognizes that he has been too long enslaved to this city; he recognizes "something finer than Athenian intellect" and he finally sails to Egypt as a member of a poetic team.

Again, Egypt complements Athens: as the continuing life of Greece was related to Hipparchia's departure for Egypt and as "The Greeks," according to the Captain in "Secret Name," "came to Egypt to learn," so in this novel, when the stranger is asked by Hedylus if he is Asiatic, he replies, "All influenced Greece is that." Individuation of personality, one may say in other words, depends upon the mind living not only in dimensions in which the rational intellect is at home but also in others where it is not. Hedyle herself has Egyptian longings in her: she wears a serpent bracelet taken from an Egyptian girl dead a thousand years. But when in the past Demion had asked her to go to Egypt, she had experienced the same sensation as Helen Fairwood encountering Egypt—of being imprisoned in a flower. She chooses not to go and the environment regains its Athenian poise: "The corridor was a whirl and then the house stood static. I recall my surprise that a room could stand so quiet, planted square on rock. A room on rock."

The novel is a bit of a mystery. What is suggested vaguely—what one supposes the devices of the novel are finally inadequate to conceive and make public—is that Hedylus and Hedyle are, by displacement, the male and female aspects of a bisexual whole and that the Athens-Egypt conflict within such a whole is resolved by the departure of the male self for Egypt.

We have seen the appeal to the living past of Caesar in Raymonde's stream of consciousness briefly illustrating one tendency of H. D.'s style. As part of the same tendency we might also notice a different kind of rehabilitation: Raymonde holds Mavis responsible for betraying Ermy as she had previously betrayed Raymonde; and the two incidents are like photographic negatives, we must suppose, superimposed upon the betrayal of H. D. herself. The internal monologue progresses, however, from simply holding Mavis guilty according to the dead Platonic precedent of "immutable laws" to bringing her alive into the present, then recreating her in Raymonde's love in the process of the creation of a poem. "Thou shalt love thy enemies. Yes, love Mavis." The alternative issues are not nakedly set forth, but we conclude that Raymonde has fished up the murex, achieved the disposition of mind that by means of charity and self-abnegation can create the poem out of the wounding experience, and that the grief is assuaged in the creation. This part of *Palimpsest* ends with the completion of her poem: "Raymonde had the last stanza—":

> with power
> I hated; see—I worship,
> more, more, more—I love her
> who has sent you to my door.
> ("Secret Name," *Palimpsest*)

Examples abound of the other tendency of style in which H. D. is apparently looking back to the past in order to find relief in its lifelessness from the constant flux of present living. In this style, even when the present is being related to it, antiquity is often presented as an immutable, Platonic form: "Antiquity endured," we learn in Raymonde's monologue, "showing flashes of pure fire-blue, temple column and gold rimmed portico behind this eternally erratic cinematograph present. . . ." In many images throughout the poetry and prose we see antiquity as a frozen scene or a static, leaf-fringed legend of unmoving figures. In her early work the H. D. of the dead classics

predominates over the one who brings them to life: in *Bid Me to Live,* Julia
says her first book of poems was made of flowers from the underworld—no
zinnias, sunflowers, or foxgloves.

Throughout much of her work, not only in her classic pieces, there is
this tendency of style to present tableaux rather than actions. Often where a
narrative contains action we find that it occurs unseen, presented to us if at
all as being just about to occur or just having occurred. Action is sometimes
barely described as such; but often H. D. avoids descriptions of movement,
presenting rather an image which in its detail gives a false sense of stasis.
There is a characteristic passage in *Hedylus:* "I always took this last jump
dubiously . . . ," the boy thinks, as he goes down to his secret beach. (The
elision marks are H. D.'s.) Then: "He landed again with firm planted feet,
with lithe heels (rigid slim twin arrows) pointed upward, with flexible sandal
toes planted firm on hard sand." Or of Hedylus again, "His small trim
sandals had trod (wild-goat-like) a little too unguardedly toward the already
crumbling wall of the Brauronia. When LYDA found him, the poppies and
his wound made one sacrificial colour against a splintered pilaster."

Passages in the poems and the novels often strike the reader as series of
stills—Hipparchia in this pose, Raymonde in that light—with carefully arranged backdrops. To anyone sufficiently curious to make it, a count would
probably reveal a high rate of copulas: "is," "seems," "recalls." In both
minor and major ways, H. D.'s style reveals the tendency to avoid the ordinary flux of life or to fix it in a static image. Thus again and again in the
novels, especially in *Hedylus,* that which is soft or fluid is rendered as hard
and fixed: the sea is repeatedly conceived as silver, or lapis, or a polished
hard floor; flesh is as marble; the curtains, porphyry; gorse blossom is gold
glass; moonlight is metallic. Things that are moving are deliberately envi-
sioned as static: in *Palimpsest,* to Marius riding with Sergius, Sergius
"scarcely seemed to swerve as his Atalanta [his horse] rocked him, cradling,
comforting like some ship at anchor. Were they there static and at anchor
in the dark plain? No whit of the landscape seemed for so many hoof-beats
to have altered." In the third section of the same novel, as the carriages throb
across the desert it seems as if they too are static: "The town drew nearer,
nearer, seeming to rush upon them, by some trick of consciousness, of itself,
as if they stood static. . . ."

The strong attraction of what is static appears in the dedicatory poem
of *Palimpsest,* addressed to Bryher, who is compared with other rare, great,
and brilliant stars and surpasses them because whereas they move she is
fixed:

when all the others, blighted, reel and fall,
your star, steel-set, keeps lone and frigid trist
to freighted ships baffled in wind and blast.
                    ("To Bryher," *Palimpsest*)

The attraction of the static is seen also in the geometrical figures that appear in the imagery, as if reality could thus be arrested or defined Platonically by appeal to an Idea behind it. There is something about regular geometrical shapes which comforts and anchors a mind confronted by the superhuman and colossal. Helen, in "Secret Name," stunned by the proportions of the palace at Karnak, takes comfort from a small birth-house, and it will be noted that she is determined to perceive things in geometric terms:

> "That little birth-house is more sizeable." She had slipped off the wall and faced it direct, at right angle to the row of bulbous columns. . . . It rose as if cut from one block of solid stone, at that little distance she could not tell of quite what material, with the moon too working its common magic, making the little tomb or outer temple look square, geometric, set square with no imperfection or break in its excellent contour, like some exquisite square of yellow honeycomb. . . . [S]he turned, having collected her flattened square fur . . . and followed Rafton across the room, the oblong room that was the banquet chamber of King Thothmes, through the arched doorway, down another path that ran parallel to the open path that had continued the line of the wall on which she had been seated.
>
>   ("Secret Name," *Palimpsest*)

The triangles and squares and circles which appear throughout the prose represent, it is fair to suggest, the urging of one part of the author's mind which accounts for one tendency of the style: the attempt to render reality in terms intellectually compassable and to harden it in its frightening mutability into recognizable shapes and patterns.

The geometric patterns appear again in the early part of *Bid Me to Live*, but less frequently in the later where Julia, the heroine, opts for the style that renders things living. The novel is set in England—during and immediately following the First World War. The narrative is seen from the point of view of Julia, a poetess and wife to Rafe Ashton, an officer serving in France, who intermittently returns on leave to London, where the first part of the novel is set. Above the Ashtons' furnished room is that of Bella Carter, an American art student, whom Rafe seduces and for whom he subsequently deserts Julia. As Rafe gradually fades out of the story, Frederick and Elsa, two characters based on D. H. Lawrence and Frieda, begin to play a larger part. They come to London, having been expelled from Cornwall. They act charades in Julia's room, and they introduce a musician called Vane, who still retains a house in Cornwall. Julia is given to understand by an equivocal gesture that Frederick loves her, but when she responds to him he is unexpectedly cool. At the end of the novel, Julia, having settled in the Cornish house with Vane, writes long letters in her notebook to Frederick, identifying him with van Gogh (on the hint of his similarity to van Gogh seen in a portrait—presumably Dorothy Brett's of Lawrence). Finally she learns that love and self-effacement—qualities which we have seen in *Palimpsest* associated with the murex—must attend a style that is to bestow life upon its subjects. The story is told from the point of view of Julia exclusively, in an impressionistic style that delights, like Ford Madox Ford's, in the breaking down of chronological sequence and, like Ford's again, in montage. Here, for instance, in part of a letter to Rico, Julia alludes to the sight of the portrait in the Bond Street window:

> What became of the dead Dutchman [van Gogh]? I know nothing at all about him, just Rafe turning off Bond Street, "We'll cut down here," and "My God, there's Rico" and "Who wants old shoes?" and "Wait here, I'll chase that taxi."
>
> (*Bid Me to Live*)

Like *Palimpsest* and *Hedylus,* the style is punctuated with repetitions.

In *Bid Me to Live,* the difference in ways of seeing experience and in matters of style is talked of in terms of dimensions. Roughly, during the London part of the novel Julia responds to the attraction of a measured world; she wants to live in a flat world, secured against vague darkness, "black nebula," as she calls it, and she partly succeeds in so doing; she resists the incursions of the additional dimension. Later, after she has ceased to live in this world, she says, "It was all flat and I loved it. . . . Then it was no longer flat but went on in different dimensions." During the second part of the novel, set in Cornwall, Julia lives in a world of another dimension: whereas in her Greek mood she had viewed experience in its measurable aspects and seen the surface level of the palimpsest, now she sees archetypes beneath immediate experience, the lower levels of the palimpsest. At the same time she claims in the later part of the novel to have rejected the style in which characters were petrified in dead classic archetypes in favor of one that permitted them to live; and it is to the matter of living that final importance is given.

The rooms Julia inhabits denote her respective states of mind. In London, the room with its two faded gilt chairs, its day-bed, the bookcase with the Elizabethan madrigals and the *Mercure de France,* the tea box with the Chinese figure on it, the gas ring, the cupboard, the Spanish screen—the room can be a paradise, a cold paradise, if the incursions of the other dimension can be withstood. And Julia loses it, even as in the charade they had all enacted, Adam and Eve lose the Garden. In this room Julia longs for clear defined things: she wants words to be finite and not echoes, she wants her husband Rafe to be the same person continuously, not a reincarnation of Marius of *Palimpsest,* a "great, over-sexed officer on leave . . . a late-Roman . . . that walked about a room, himself with no clothes on." One night Rafe mutters, and she wonders whether he is dreaming or making it up: "Did he want to make this up, to ruin what she had so carefully preserved, the fact of this room, the continuity of this bed, the presence of herself, the same self beside him?"

In the room there are defenses against discontinuity: the continuous existence of its furniture, for example, the items of which are named repeatedly; the continual smoking of cigarettes; the little watch that Rafe gave to Julia on returning to France after leave. There is security, too, even in the heart of a destructive situation, in viewing things according to a geometrical pattern. In the following, *l'autre* refers to Bella, and "the time" refers to Rafe's leave:

> *L'autre* was out on the wild or *l'autre* was alone upstairs, maybe even now waiting for Rafe to join her. Oh, it was all a muddle. But no, it was not. There was the candle and its exact circle of light, an exact geometrical definition, as exact as the clock-dial on the clock, as the little circle on the watch he had strapped round her wrist, the time before the time before the last.
>
> (*Bid Me to Live*)

The security bestowed by geometry had comforted her earlier when sketching a bridge in Paris:

> She blocked round it, it gave her a sense of continuity, it gave her her own proportion, placed her in the centre of a circle, which she measured, mock-professionally, with a pencil held before her. When she squinted at the pencil, she was not so much seeing the thing she was about to block in roughly, as making a circle, with a compass, for herself to stay in.
>
> (*Bid Me to Live*)

Life might be controlled by limiting it in a plane geometric figure or, for that matter, in a painting, if only it did not elude this treatment. So Rico might capture Bella in part, but there was more than could be rendered in a candy-box type of painting. He "put her on the map"

> with his *fleur-de-pêche* [his name for her makeup] and calling her mother *entrepreneuse*. But there was more to it than just that. Rico made neat pictures, put Bella on a band-box, painted her on a fan. But opening the fan, there were other dimensions, layers of poison-gas, the sound of shrapnel, the motto that ran across the top of the fan when it was spread open was *I have a rendez-vous with death*.
>
> (*Bid Me to Live*)

There are also explicit dangers to the room and the continuity it fosters: the air raids, which send the books flying out of the shelves; somewhat obviously, the use of the bed by Rafe and Bella; parties—"parties certainly had smashed what lines had been left in the air by the casual reading of *Hesperides*."

This room was always cold. But at one point in the novel the cold is unusually emphasized: Julia waits for Rafe to come down from Bella's flat to say goodbye. There are winter hyacinths; "She wore the blue corduroy-velvet that fell, they said, like Parthenon folds, its corduroy-velvet lines giving, they had said, a Greek line"; the whole passage that describes the occasion is punctuated by the phrase, "very cold, very old." This is the climax of Julia's career in the Greek dimension, living in the set of measured terms; and it is the last scene in the London room. Coming to live in Cornwall does not make a sudden change in her view, however, for there have been all along times when life has taken on the complications of depth. There are, as noted, the unwelcome occasions when its continuity has been disturbed. But all such occasions are not unwelcome: with Rico, one might get "past the point of any logic and of any meaning" to another where "everything has a meaning. A meaning in another dimension, not even that." Things may obtain meaning by being seen superimposed upon one another:

> Elsa's work-bag spilling its homely contents on the floor, Rico looking for a pen-knife, Bella twisting a ribbon for a hat on the chintz-covered settee. . . . Hold them up to the light and you get in reverse light-and-shade, Julia and Bella seated on that same chintz-covered couch, a composite, you get Rico seated in Rafe's arm-chair, you get Elsa, Germania, in its largest proportion, su-perimposed simply on Rule Britannia.
>
> (*Bid Me to Live*)

Or again, though she has nothing in common with Bella, Julia feels when facing her that she was looking at herself in the mirror—"another self, another dimension. . . ." Or when the World War presses close and seems to threaten the continuity of life, Julia retreats to "another dimension," in which she lives a dream life, in love with Rico, quite withdrawn from the room.

The high point among these London experiences in the added dimension is the occasion when Vane takes Julia to the cinema to see a romance, set in the Italian mountains. Julia identifies the heroine of the film with Venus, Persephone, and Primavera, implicitly recognizing the possibility of the reincarnation of these mythical characters, holding them not dead but living, moving figures. She identifies herself with the heroine on the screen and hence with the classic figures; later she again sees herself as Persephone: we have an instance of the kind of vision that H. D. associates with the palimpsest.

It was Rico who had introduced Vane to her; and it is thus indirectly through his agency that she sees the film and then consequently decides to go to Cornwall, though Rico exhibits the old Laurentian puritanism at the prospect of her sharing the cottage with a man. Cornwall opens her mind to the new dimension: the past seems but a dream compared with this new reality, where the whole environment is symbolic, mythical parallels suggest themselves, and things are "racially remembered." She has left the old room behind with its agents of continuity—"the rumpled bed, the unwashed teacups, the ash-tray heaped with cigarette-ends"; and once again we see a heroine crouched like an insect before immensity: "She hugged her old coat tight, hugging herself tight, rejoicing in herself, butterfly in cocoon."

If there is an actual moment of change, however, it is presumably marked by Julia's symbolic move within the Cornish cottage into a room with two doors. At first, upon arrival, she does not have this room; and her occupation of it marks a turning point occasioned also by three other factors: she has left off working on a Greek chorus sequence; second, she has started to write to Rico; third, in her own words, she has begun "to think of Vincent van Gogh." Her dropping of the Greek chorus sequence marks a departure in her poetic style: she had thought as she worked on the Greek that she would have to work forever "to hew and chisel those lines, to maintain or suggest some cold artistry." Van Gogh represents painting in a third dimension: his pictures are not in one plane but "dynamically exploding inside." About her change of room she says, "Everything is different since I moved."

The kind of art she now admires is what she feels Rico has achieved, if not in his novels at least in his letters to her, and what she wishes to achieve herself. Its important property is that it makes people live (or lets them); it does not render them up as cold artifacts or abstractions. Julia writes to Rico, "You jeered at my making abstractions of people—graven images, you called them. You are right." The magic tincture of the style seems to be self-effacement: Vane calls Julia "Person," which she equates with the French *personne*, nobody. At least passiveness is an important ingredient, like that which Hipparchia possesses in her Egyptian mood: "All endeavour was (by her new standard) misdirected."

In the second part of *Palimpsest* the murex is the agency that will transform experience into poetry. Now at the end of H. D.'s last novel, Julia speaks not of murex but of *gloire*, the word being taken (arbitrarily) from a poem by Rico (and Lawrence) about Gloire de Dijon roses. *Gloire* is the potential of the art about to be created—"The child is the *gloire* before it is born. The circle of the candle on my notebook is the *gloire*, the story isn't born yet."

"While I live in the unborn story, I am in the *gloire*." The emphasis at last falls not on what one must do to achieve a style but on what the achieved style can do for its owner. If in the act of creation the style calls for negation of self, *gloire* implies full restoration of the self in the created art. "When I try to explain," says Julia, "I write the story. The story must write *me*, the story must create *me*. . . . He [van Gogh] would get into the cypress tree, through his genius, through his daemon. . . . It is worship. . . ." Later, "Vincent is in the cypress, he is in the blossoming fruit-tree, he is in the *gloire*."

The novels repeat with variations the predicament of a woman dispossessed of husband or lover, who emerges from her loss with two alternative ways of dealing with experience: there is the way of cold finite intellection on the part of the active ego, which seeks stability in the flux of living by reducing it to dead, frozen scenes poised for eternity; or there is the imprecise vision informed by reflections from the past not of such scenes but of living models of people and of experience to be endlessly recreated. Before this kind of vision the active thinking self shrinks into a wise passiveness only to find itself again flourishing within a created work of art.

SUSAN FRIEDMAN

Who Buried H. D.?
A Poet, Her Critics, and Her Place
in "The Literary Tradition"

H. D. is a major twentieth-century poet who all too often receives the
response "H. D.?—who's he?" When people are reminded that "H. D." was
the pen name for Hilda Doolittle, it is generally remembered that she was
one of those imagist poets back in the beginning of the century who changed
the course of modern poetry with their development of the "image" and free
verse. Her early poems, like "Oread" or "Heat," still appear regularly in
modern poetry anthologies, but the more difficult epic poetry she went on
to write is seldom studied or taught. The canon of her major, largely unread
work is considerable: *The Walls Do Not Fall* (1944), *Tribute to the Angels*
(1945), and *The Flowering of the Rod* (1946) are the three long poems of
her war *Trilogy*, which has recently been reissued; *Helen in Egypt* (1961) is
the work she called her own "Cantos"; the newly published volume *Hermetic
Definition* (1972) contains three more long poems, the title poem, *Winter
Love*, and *Sagesse*; and *Vale Ave* is another, as-yet-unpublished epic poem.
While poetry was undoubtedly the genre giving fullest expression to her
creative energies, she also published numerous translations, acted in a movie
whose script she wrote (*Borderline*, with Paul Robeson, 1930), experimented
with drama (*Hippolytus Temporizes*, 1927), and wrote several novels (*Hedylus*, 1928; *Palimpsest*, 1926; *Bid Me to Live (A Madrigal)*, 1960; and the
largely unpublished *The Gift*), interesting at the very least for her own style
of rendering stream of consciousness. Her memoir of Freud, *Tribute to Freud*

From *College English* 36, no. 7 (March 1975). © 1975 by the National Council of
Teachers of English.

(1956), is both an impressionistic record of their sessions together and a serious reevaluation of his impact on the twentieth century; it too has been recently reissued in expanded form. Caged in a literary movement that lasted all of six or seven years, the magnificent poet of these epics and the writer who experimented in a wide variety of genres is like the captured white-faced Scops owl in her poem *Sagesse*. While the onlookers at the zoo chatter about his comical whiskers and baggy trousers, the owl who is both the embodiment of divinity and the personification of the poet is "a captive and in prison":

> You look at me, a hut or cage contains
> your fantasy, your frantic stare;
>
> . . . .
>
> May those who file before you feel
> something of what you are
>
> . . . .
>
> they will laugh and linger and some child may shudder,
>
> touched by the majesty, the lifted wings,
> the white mask and the eyes that seem to see,
>
> like God, everything and like God, see nothing.

As Hugh Kenner wrote in his review of *Hermetic Definition*, to identify H. D. as an imagist poet is "as though five of the shortest pieces in 'Harmonium' were to stand for the life's work of Wallace Stevens" (*New York Times Book Review*, December 10, 1972). But if H. D. is not already buried in a single moment of literary history, she is rapidly becoming so.

Why is her poetry not read? H. D. is part of the same literary tradition that produced the mature work of the "established artists"—T. S. Eliot, Ezra Pound, William Carlos Williams, D. H. Lawrence. She in fact knew these artists well; she had known and almost married Pound while the two were students in Philadelphia (H. D.'s intensely absorbing recreation of their life-time friendship, *End to Torment*, is being prepared for publication); her friendship with Williams goes back to those student days; but most important, she was an active member of the London literary circle that spun out the dazzling succession of artistic "isms"—imagism, dadaism, vorticism, futurism—before the catastrophe of the First World War smashed this coterie into the confusion of a spiritual wasteland. Like these artists, H. D. began writing in the aestheticism and fascination for pure form characteristic of the imagists; and like them, she turned to epic form and to myth, religious tradition, and the dream as a way of giving meaning to the cataclysms and fragmentation of the twentieth century. Her epic poetry should be compared to the *Cantos, Paterson,* the *Four Quartets,* and *The Bridge,* for like these poems, her work is the kind of "cosmic poetry" the imagists swore they would never write.

The pattern of her poetic development not only paralleled that of more famous artists, but it was also permeated by major intellectual currents of the century. In 1933 and 1934 she was psychoanalyzed by Freud, an exploration deep within her own unconscious that ultimately linked for her the personal with the universal, the private myth with the "tribal" myths. At the same time that she studied with Freud, the convinced materialist, she was a student of comparative religion, of esoteric tradition, and, like Yeats, of the occult. The forces perpetually at work to bring a directionless century to war were a constant preoccupation in her work. Consciously rejecting the mechanistic, materialist conceptions of reality that formed the faith of the empirical modern age, H. D. affirmed a "spiritual realism" and the relevance of a quest for intangible meanings. Her growth into a poet exploring the psyche or soul of humanity and reaching out to confront the questions of history, tradition, and myth places her squarely in the mainstream of "established" modern literature. But still, outside of a few poets like Denise Levertov, who wrote "An Appreciation" of H. D., Robert Duncan, and the afficionados who circulate a pirated edition of *Hermetic Definition,* few people read her poetry. Once again, why?

Is her poetry just plain "bad," however serious the philosophic and human issues she embodies in image and epic narration? For me, the answer is obvious—her poems captivate, enchant, and enlighten me. From my single, necessarily subjective perspective, there is no doubt that her poetry is magnificent. But I have no intention here of raising the thorny questions of what makes literature "great," who determines the standards for greatness, or even whether the literary reputation of an author has much of anything to do with genuine genius. I do insist, however, that H. D. was a serious prolific poet exploring the same questions as her famous counterparts and thus inviting comparison with them. It is something of an understatement, I think, to say that in our profession artists do not have to wear the badge of greatness in order to have articles and books written about them. The simple relevance of her work to the issues and experiments of modern poetry demands that it be studied. And so I am still asking why H. D.'s work is buried under a scattered knowledge of "Oread" or "Heat."

The answer is simple enough, I think. It lies biographically and factually right in front of our critical noses—too close perhaps to be seen easily. It lies in what makes H. D. and her work different from a long string of more studied poets like Eliot, Pound, Crane, Williams, and Yeats. And it lies in the response of her critics. She was a woman, she wrote about women, and all the ever-questioning, artistic, intellectual heroes of her epic poetry and novels were women. In the quest poetry and fiction of the established literary tradition (particularly the poetic tradition), women as active, thinking, individual human beings rarely exist. They are instead the apocalyptic Pocahontas and the demonic prostitute of *The Bridge,* the goddess in the park sought by the poet Paterson, the superficial women walking to and fro talking of Michelangelo. They are the static, symbolic objects of quest, not the questors; they are "feminine principles," both threatening and life-giving, and not particularized human beings. Women are dehumanized, while the quest of the male poet is presented and understood as the anguished journey of the prophet-seer for the absolute on behalf of all humankind. For "mankind" they may be the spokesmen, but for "womenkind" they are not. As a woman writing about women, H. D. explored the untold half of the human story, and by that act she set herself outside of the established tradition. She became a "woman poet" in a world in which the word "poet" actually means male poet and the word "mankind" too often includes only men. From this perspective there are poets, and then there are the lady poets, or poetesses; there are people, and then there are women.

If her sex and her women subjects were not enough to exile her from the roster of the literary establishment, the response of many critics to her epic poetry completed the process. Her critics have rarely forgotten that she was a woman writing poetry. And I don't think they should have forgotten that fundamental fact. But her appearance in criticism as "woman poet" is never positive as it should be; it becomes instead the subtle ground on which she can be ultimately ignored. Elaborate intellectual scaffolds resting on the fact of her sex have been constructed by some of her critics whose net effect has been to dismiss her.

I will be concrete. In 1969 a special issue of *Contemporary Literature* was devoted to H. D. after years of critical silence about her work. It was the hope of L. S. Dembo, *Contemporary Literature*'s editor, who had recently published a serious chapter introducing her late poetry, that this special issue would spark renewed interest in her work. It did not. Aside from two fine reviews of her new publications, no articles or books have followed. Her later poetry is rarely studied in the universities; and she is not even appearing in the wonderfully useful bibliographies of forgotten literature written by women and the new anthologies of rediscovered women writers (Florence Howe's *No More Masks!* is an exception).

Looking at the first two articles in *Contemporary Literature*'s special issue—and they are both long, serious, thoroughly researched articles by well-known scholars, Joseph N. Riddel and Norman N. Holland—I am not surprised that it produced more critical silence instead of new studies. Riddel in his "H. D. and the Poetics of 'Spiritual Realism'" and Holland in his "H. D. and the 'Blameless Physician'" take as their starting point H. D.'s psychoanalysis with Freud and her book about that experience. Holland and Riddel are absolutely correct in pointing to that experience as the key to her poetry. But in their hands this valuable key ends up locking the doors to our understanding instead of opening them as it can do.

Although Holland and Riddel dutifully quote some of her careful statements in *Tribute to Freud*—and they are as careful as Thoreau's in *Walden*—about why she went to talk with Freud, their basic analysis (particularly Riddel's) ignores what she said about how she went to Freud as his "student," his "disciple," about how she saw psychoanalysis as a medium of quest in a drifting century, about how she found with his guidance the way to link her personal past with that of people in all places, at all times. Refusing to take seriously H. D.'s own comments about the impact of Freud on her artistic identity, Riddel and Holland dissect her with all the Freudian terminology they can muster—as if she were a neurotic woman, a "patient" instead of the artist who warned her readers that "in our talks together he [Freud] rarely used any of the now rather overworked technical terms, invented by himself and elaborated on by the growing body of doctors, psychologists and nerve specialists." And, we might add, literary critics. Holland explicitly and Riddel implicitly start with Freud's statement that a woman's "strongest motive in coming for treatment was the hope that, after all, she might still obtain a male organ, the lack of which was so painful to her" (Holland). For these critics, a central issue of H. D.'s psychoanalysis is "penis envy"—in Riddel's article, it is *the* central issue; in Holland's essay, penis envy shares the stage with the longing to fuse with her mother, a carryover from the oral phase. But even more destructively, in their discussion of her psyche as the generating source in her art, H. D.'s supposedly self-evident longing for a penis (don't all women want one?) becomes the focus for their discussion of her artistic identity and poetry.

Riddel, like Freud, reduces the psychology of women to a physiological level, seeing the woman's genitals as the fundamental metaphor of what *he* calls "feminine incompleteness," "inwardness," "subjectivity," and "softness" and measuring her anatomy against a male standard of power and sufficiency, the penis. Just as Freud refers in his own voice to a girl's clitoris as a "stunted penis," Riddel writes about H. D. as "phallus-less," having an "ontological deprivation." "Suffocating" from her "feminine inwardness,"

Riddel concludes, H. D. turned to the hard, male objectivity of myth, poetic form, and symbolic objects (Riddel's subjective assumption that poetic form and art objects are male is not even Freudian; it contradicts what many Freudians argue: that artistic "forms" are "vessels" and represent the artists' oral wish to reunite with the mother).

While Holland is more likely than Riddel to use the careful language of H. D.'s perceptions ("again, we seem to be coming to the theme of overcompensating for what *she feels* is the inferior quality of her feminine body," my italics), his basic thesis is still that H. D.'s creative expressions are evidence for her perpetual search for the "masculinity" which was "lost" or "missing" in the first place. At the same time that she sought through therapy to "close the gap" between herself and her mother (oral stage), she transferred to Freud all the "phallic power" she had attributed to her father and her brother (phallic and oedipal stages). In the transference H. D. was able to absorb some of Freud's masculine power ("Fusion with a man insures against deficiency: thus H. D. found it easy to project into and identify with Freud"). Her poetry, with its reliance on "hard" "signs," completed the process she had begun with Freud of closing up the gaps in her body as well as her consciousness.

Both critics conclude that H. D.'s infantile wishes were resolved in therapy as Freud succeeded in rooting out her penis envy, in teaching her to accept her "feminine incompleteness," in giving her "the ability to live in her wingless self " and to discover her "woman's role." Ignoring H. D.'s own interpretation of the "wingless Niké"—wingless in myth so that Victory can never fly away from Athens, a positive symbol of hope for H. D.—the critics change it into the phallus-less, powerless woman. Freud's gift to H. D. was to resign her to the fact of her winglessness, her femininity.

Yet once having argued that Freud successfully convinced H. D. that she was a woman, both critics somewhat inconsistently conclude that H. D.'s poetry was a product of her unresolved penis envy. Holland writes finally that her poems are the legacy of her continuing search for those "missing things." He generously concludes:

> I feel sadness for a woman who had to become a royal and mythic sign [he refers to her use of her initials as a pen name and her portrayal of her women heroes as "hieroglyphs"] to make up for all those missing things. But I honor the poet. She did indeed close up the gap with signs and, in doing so, left to us a body of poems for which we can be grateful.
> (Holland, "H. D. and the 'Blameless Physician,'" *Contemporary Literature*)

Riddel stresses the inherent difficulty all women have in creating an artistic identity:

> The identity of the creative self as woman is threatened not only by the incompleteness of the female but by the insubstantiality of subjectivity. . . . In terms of the self-consciousness that forces her to contemplate her ambiguous role as woman poet, she seeks the conpleteness of the subject in the object. She must turn herself into a poem.
>   (Riddel, "H. D. and the Poetics of 'Spiritual Realism,'"
>   *Contemporary Literature*)

And since the poem is designated objective and "male" in Riddel's scheme of things, he argues implicitly that H. D. must abandon her identity as a woman if she is to develop as a poet. For Riddel, not only are poems masculine, but myths, symbols, and cult objects are linked with the "phallus . . . the signifier, the giver of meaning" (Riddel). By what yardstick Riddel measures things like words or myths as penis-connected or masculine, he never says. But identify the tools of an artist's trade and the kind of images H. D. chose with all that's masculine, Riddel definitely does do. He comes as close as any critic to affirming that the province of the poet is entirely masculine and the woman poet who succeeds in writing poetry must overcome, destroy, or transcend her femininity and write like a man.

For all that the general tone of his essay appears to be detached, scholarly, and objective, Riddel's assumptions about women and women poets color and often distort his discussion of her epic poetry. Her impulse to write poetry—to handle words, to create images—originates in his perspective in her recognition of the inferiority of women and the superiority of men, in short, in penis envy. And the epic poetry of her later years which shows a turning to myth and the imagery of sacred cult objects—poetry that Riddel discusses brilliantly if his psychoanalytic framework is ignored—emerges out of her anguished search for masculine objectivity. Riddel has reduced the creative urge and poetic vision of H. D. to her desire to have what any ordinary man, poet or not, possesses from birth.

Is it any wonder that Riddel's and Holland's descriptions of H. D.'s quest for the phallus have not stimulated renewed interest in her work? Why should anyone bother reading a poet in search of "masculine hardness" when you can take your pick from among any number of "hard" male poets?

Although the work of these two critics has angered me greatly, both as a woman and as a person who sees H. D.'s poetry unjustly treated, my point is not to attack the criticism of individuals. I am far more concerned with

the general issue of what impact the male-oriented criticism of modern schol-
arship has had on the literary reputations of women writers like H. D. I am
interested in Riddel's and Holland's articles for their blatant documentation
of the fact that criticism is written from a subjective male point of view;
that, no matter how scholarly and well-researched such articles may be, they
are not value-free.

While Riddel tends to present himself as an objective scholar, Holland
himself would not disagree that all criticism is subjective. In fact, the central
argument of his newest book, *Poems in Persons,* is that *all* literary experiences—including the logical, careful, internally coherent work of literary
critics—are necessarily subjective. But what he means by "subjectivity" (the
recreation of a literary work within the terms of an individual reader's "ego
identity," his or her uniquely woven pattern of childhood psychosexual fantasy) is not at all what I mean. His own "subjective" viewpoint which colors
so much of what he writes about H. D. is instead a misogynist set of psychoanalytic presuppositions about the infantile wishes of young girls which
he takes to be "objective" truth. This type of political and cultural subjectivity that so pervades Holland's and Riddel's work is symptomatic of the
prejudiced inadequacies of much literary criticism, non-psychoanalytic as
well as that heavily influenced by Freud.

I can hear voices objecting to my generalization—you are making a
mountain out of a mole hill; Riddel and Holland are only two men; dismiss
them as male critics and get back to the business of criticism. It is true that
by themselves they are only two men; but if they are pushed to the side as
exceptions—rather than seen as examples of a hidden pattern set in bold
relief—the main body of criticism can continue to put forth its mask of
scholarly objectivity. In their criticism of H. D.'s works they are not simply
exceptions to a generally fair rule; perhaps because of their psychoanalytic
interests, their work is a more explicit version of the double standard in
criticism. Vincent Quinn, for example, wrote a generally useful book on
H. D., *Hilda Doolittle* (1967), that focuses mainly on her imagist poetry.
But a subtler form of male perspective is evident in his discussion of her epic
poetry. He provides a good introduction to the religious, prophetic vision of
the war *Trilogy*—he has understood what her work is about—but he is
entirely uncomfortable with it. It is too abstract, too philosophical; its the-
ology, based on a belief in the essential oneness of divinity throughout all
cultures, is confusing. As a writer of short, lyric, emotional poems about
nature, love, and beauty, H. D. was at her best, in Quinn's opinion. But a
double standard of judgment for men and women writers may have something to do with Quinn's evaluation of H. D.'s poetry. H. D.'s compatriots,

Eliot, Williams, and Pound, left the imagist poem to write epics permeated with mythological and religious allusions and with complex philosophical abstractions; yet they are praised for the profundity of their poetic thought and not accused of abstraction. In fact, none of her late work, which always has a highly personal as well as a mythic dimension, is as abstract as a poem like the *Four Quartets*. But subtle enough so that even Quinn might not have been aware of his own assumptions may be the feeling that H. D.'s work was too abstract for a woman to write. The short, passionate lyric has conventionally been thought appropriate for women poets if they insist on writing, while the longer, more philosophic epic belongs to the real (male) poet. Perhaps it is this presupposition about women writers that has caused so many of H. D.'s critics (see Douglas Bush and Thomas Swann, for example) to label her interest in mythology "escapist." Even Linda Welshimer Wagner (women, too, can analyze from the male perspective—that has been, after all, our training), who has some interesting comments to make on "the feminine" in *Helen in Egypt*, saw H. D.'s fascination with myth as a search for "solace" and escape. When Eliot, Pound, Williams, and Yeats show that same rejection of materialist conceptions of reality, they are praised for their struggle to deal with the ultimate questions of human existence. It is a kind of double talk emerging out of a hidden bias that makes Eliot deeply religious, Pound profound, Crane prophetic, Williams archetypal, and Yeats visionary while the same phenomenon in H. D. is "escapist." If there is to be any growth in the understanding of literature by women, or by any other group not accepted within the recognized literary tradition, or even by the established artists, these hidden biases and the necessarily subjective nature of all criticism (as all art) must be confronted.

H. D.'s poetry itself brings into bold relief the assumptions of her critics that have been so damaging to her reputation. Her own explorations of women's experience and the dilemma of women writers correct, more eloquently than I can, the mistaken prejudices of her critics and the distorting lens of a double standard for men and women writers. Riddel's and Holland's Freudian conception of a woman torn with desire to possess the penis—or at any rate something "hard"—is nowhere demonstrated in the "woman's epic" that H. D. writes. Missing also are various other critical assumptions they make: that H. D. found her fulfillment as a woman by resignation to "winglessness"; that the "phallic" and the "masculine" are associated with power, myth, poetry, objectivity, and meaning in opposition to the "feminine" qualities of weakness, softness, insubstantiality, subjectivity; and so forth. The more diffused, less psychoanalytic, description of the mature poet as a fragile naiad escaping into the still world of an imaginary Greece bears no relationship to the H. D. who used myth to confront the most contemporary and timeless problems in women's lives. Even less do H. D.'s women heroes fit the stereotypes of women in the kitchens of the world or in the poetry of male poets.

   Winter Love (Espérance), a newly published poem of H. D.'s (continuing in twenty-eight sections the quest of Helen in *Helen in Egypt*), demonstrates forcefully how distant the stereotypes and conventions of literature and the complementary distortions of criticism often are from the reality of a woman's perspective. Helen of Troy, that symbol of dangerous love and beauty in so many poems by male poets, is in H. D.'s poem not a distant symbol, nor some soft creature seeking to fuse with some male hero, nor a reflection of H. D.'s willingness to accept her "ontological deprivation." Listen instead to the woman's anguish in the final section of *Winter Love* as Helen gives birth to her child Espérance and recalls the succession of lovers who have come in and gone out of her life:

> I am delirious now and mean to be,
> the whole earth shudders with my ecstacy,
> take Espérance away;
>
> cruel, cruel *Sage-Femme*,
> to place him in my arms,
> cruel, cruel *Grande Dame*,
>
> to pull my tunic down,
> so Odysseus sought my breast
> with savage kiss;
>
> cruel, cruel midwife,
> so secretly to steal my phantom self,
> my invisibility, my hopelessness, my fate
>
> the guilt, the blame, the desolation,
> Paris slain to rise again
> and find Oenone and mortality,
>
> Achilles' flight to Thetis
> and the Sea (deserting *Leuké*),
> Menelaus with his trophies in the palace,
>
> Odysseus—take the Child away,
> cruel, cruel is Hope,
> terrible the weight of honey and of milk,

Cruel, cruel, the thought of Love,
while Helen's breasts swell, painful
with the ambrosial sap, *Amrita*

that must be given;
I die in agony whether I give or do not give;
cruel, cruel *Sage-Femme*,

wiser than all the regents of God's throne,
why do you torture me?
come, come O *Espérance*,

Espérance, O golden bee,
take life afresh and if you must,
so slay me.

(Winter Love)

In this moment of delirium, when the aging Helen sees the lovers of her life pass before her—Paris at Troy, Achilles in Egypt and Leuké, Menelaus back in Sparta, and finally Odysseus, the father of Espérance—she is left with "my phantom self, / my invisibility, my hopelessness, my fate, / the guilt, the blame, the desolation." She is a woman used—sought in violence by Odysseus; abandoned finally by Paris, who returns to his first love Oenone; and Achilles, who deserts Helen for his mother Thetis (Menelaus is something of a bore with his trophies and stale stories). And is the child Espérance consolation for the emptiness of life that has left her clinging to the only identity she has—"my phantom self, / my invisibility?" Is he, in Freudian terms, the satisfying sublimation for penis envy? "The whole earth shudders with my ecstasy"; Helen cannot help but feel joy in the overwhelming experience of the birth, but mixed with this "ecstasy" is great pain, for the Child, with the added irony of his name, Hope, brings a special agony. Helen sees him as linked to the older men who took from her and fled: "cruel, cruel, *Grande Dame*, / to pull my tunic down, / so Odysseus sought my breast / with savage kiss." For, like a lover, the Child demands and she must give. She is not even to be left in peace with her "phantom self," a kind of death itself (see section 27 of *Winter Love*), but at least her own. To the Child she must give milk—"while Helen's breasts swell, painful / with the ambrosial sap, *Amrita* / that must be given"; to deny the baby is torture, to give all he demands is agony: "I die in agony whether I give or do not give." The Child, in taking milk and love from his mother, is bringing a kind of death upon her: "Espérance, O golden bee, / take life afresh and if you must, / so slay me." The special cruelty is that the birth of this child should be, as his name suggests, a woman's hope, but the Child's all-encompassing demands mean death for Helen because once again she will have to give and give and give, only to be left by the grown child in the end: "take the Child away, / cruel, cruel, is Hope // cruel, cruel the thought of Love." Yet, as with her lovers, she finally puts the Child's needs before her own; Helen's cry in the middle of the poem to "take the Child away, / cruel, cruel, is Hope," becomes by the end "come, come, O Espérance" as she welcomes the new-born to her breast.

Rather than suggesting consoling escape from reality, rather than representing the acquisition of "phallic objectivity," the mythic dimension of the poem adds cruel irony to the agony of this woman, to this poetic version of postpartum depression. From the time of Homer to the twentieth century Helen has been the symbol of woman in her most perfect form. Yet this poem with Helen as the subjective voice instead of the object of some poet's glazed eyes reveals desperate unhappiness. The "Sage-Femme" (literally "mid-wife" in French), the "Grande Dame," who brings the child safely to term and into the world is not worshipped here by Helen as the Great Earth Mother—she is "cruel," all the more so because she and Helen are both women, sisters. And capitalization of "Child" makes explicit the parallel between Helen-Espérance and Mary-Jesus, Isis-Horus, and all the other mother figures in mythology and art. Yet instead of reveling in this mythic parallel, instead of celebrating her fulfillment as a woman, Helen cries out in agony as she once again witnesses the death of her individual self. H. D. is not writing about Helen of Troy, however; we shouldn't let the poem's ancient speaker and this whole mythic dimension interfere with the direct, contemporary, universal voice of the poem—the agony of a middle-aged woman who has given and cannot stop giving to her lovers and her children. H. D.'s poem is all about women who are driven to fulfill others' demands only to find themselves left with a "phantom self," an "invisibility," a "hope-lessness."

The woman in *Winter Love* is lamenting "missing things," but not the missing penis of Holland's analysis. Throughout all the sections of the poem, as in many of H. D.'s epics, she searches for the missing identity, for a direction and purpose which is so often denied to women. Caught within the Freudian or even more generally male-oriented categories of her critics, this theme of missing identity or "invisibility" in the midst of love and birth could easily be twisted into evidence for the persistence of H. D.'s unresolved phallic stage, for her desire to flee "feminine inwardness," or for her attempt to acquire power by merging with a man and with the "phallic signifiers" of knowledge. But such readings would be a total distortion of what H. D.

is saying—about how that "phallic power" has presented Helen with a life-time of demands, only to desert the drained phantom in the end; about how the ecstasy of birth is mingled with the recognition of a death of the individual self. Freed from the confines of a critical cage, this poem clearly contradicts the kinds of assumptions H. D.'s critics have made as they approach her work.

Perhaps, however, my reading of one small section of only one poem by H. D. is too limited an example upon which to rest my case that a male-oriented bias has had dire consequences in the understanding of H. D.'s poetry. What about the whole sweep of her epic quests? Do they bear out my contention that H. D. has set herself outside the established literary tradition by her exploration of human experience from a woman's perspective and that conventional male categories of literary criticism must be abandoned if her work is to be understood? The thematic thrust and "arguments" of her major poems do indeed reveal how misleading some of her critics have been. In the war *Trilogy*, written as the German bombs created a crucible of fire out of her home, and in *Helen in Egypt*, written a few years later in quiet reflection on a war-torn century, H. D. expresses a vision in total opposition to envy for the male world. Both epics are poetic arguments for a belief similar to Carolyn Heilbrun's in *Towards a Recognition of Androgyny:* the dominance of masculine values has brought destruction and suffering, like the catastrophe of the two world wars. The "phallus" and its weaponed manifestations are never the "signifiers" of meaning as Riddel rather self-importantly suggests; they have been instead the destroyers of human potentiality.

In *Helen in Egypt* Achilles represents the "Whirlwind of War" as the leader of the "warrior cults" of the "purely masculine iron-ring." It is *he* who must learn from Helen how his sword "has blighted that peace" embodied in the Goddess and how he can become the "new Mortal" by recapturing the feminine values of union and creation represented in his past by his mother Thetis and in the present by Helen herself. Even more explicitly in the war *Trilogy*, H. D. resurrects the powerful ancient deities of the matriarchies whom she associates with the positive values of love, peace, regeneration, and synthesis as the poet transforms degraded "venery" into "veneration" for Venus, Aphrodite, Isis—the Lady or female principle in general. In both epics these active, powerful forces of birth and reintegration are scarcely similar to the placid, fecund goddesses awaiting some lance-carrying hero for fulfillment that abound in the patriarchal mythologies and literature. And they bear little resemblance to Riddel's portrayal of "soft," "weak" femininity seeking escape into the strength of whatever he happens to label "masculine." In fact both epics attempt to transcend the divisions into male and female as they reach for a vision of individual identity, society, and religion based on an androgynous union of the strongest and most creative aspects of the traditionally "masculine" and "feminine." In so doing they reveal a writer who believes that to rectify the understanding of women's experience and matriarchal values leads the poet-prophet to confront universal questions of history, time, and humanity.

The last poem the aging, ailing poet wrote, the recently published *Hermetic Definition,* sharply focuses the broader issues explored in the earlier epics to a highly personal account of the dilemma faced by the woman poet. As she tries to combine the woman in love and the woman at work into a single artistic identity, her difficulties are great, as Holland and Riddel suggested they would be. But totally inconsistent with her final resolution are both Holland's description of the "ego theme" by which she writes poetry to acquire the power she associated with a whole string of male figures since childhood, and Riddel's contention that H. D. had to transcend her femininity to write like a man. The poem is first of all an implicit rejection of a Freudian tenet that infuses both Holland's and Riddel's work and our culture in general. Freud saw an unbridgeable chasm separating the "masculine" woman—the active, competitive woman whose early development was "arrested" in penis envy and its consequent sublimation into all sorts of "male" activities, and the "feminine" woman—the passive, weak woman who had passed beyond penis envy into an acceptance of her domestic role. In Freud's eyes and within the perspective of the generally acceptable attitudes which Freud's "science" did so much to legitimize, a woman is simply not expected to be capable of both the joys of love and motherhood and the rigors of work beyond the home. Yet H. D. in the poem, as in so much of her work, portrays a woman poet simultaneously passionate in her love for a man and in her commitment to write poetry.

The poet's search is not for a man to fuse with or be like—it is precisely the opposite: the process of the poem's quest is how to escape from the influence of two men in order to find her own vision and direction. One man is Lionel Durand, who represents for H. D. the Lover and the Son and whom she actually met when he came to interview her for a *Newsweek* review of her novel *Bid Me to Live.* At age seventy H. D. fell electrically in love with Durand, and was in fact obsessed with this love for the nine months it took her to write the poem, as her diary of the period reflects. But both in her life and in the poem Durand rejected H. D., as a woman and as a poet. His personal letters to her were polite and distant; her work, he wrote, was "fascinating if you can stand its 'preciousness' " (*H. D.*). To deny his condemnation of her work she listens to the voice of her guide, her Muse—once again the powerful female deity and patron of the mysteries, not any representative of the "phallus" or "masculine" objectivity: Isis "draws the veil aside, / unbinds my eyes, / commands / write, write or die" (*H. D.*). In contrast to Riddel's description of the ambivalence of her role as a woman writer, H. D. writes about the problem of many women writers—the ridicule they receive from their critics and reviewers.

Rejection by Durand leads H. D. into an intense study of the hermetic poetry of St. John Perse. As she is entranced with Perse's philosophic, esoteric vision and his acceptance of her as a poet, she gradually comes to realize that she must pass beyond the poetry of Perse to find her own way, one which will "recover the human equation," the human experience of her love for Durand, a dimension which is missing from Perse's more abstract, more "formal and external" (*H. D.*) poetry. She cannot rely on any man to be her voice. To insure herself against "deficiency," to echo Holland, she must speak for herself and avoid fusion with a man, lover, or fellow poet. Her symbolic expression of her successful independence is this poem itself, whose writing she images as a pregnancy and a final painful birth. Such a metaphor for poetic creation has been somewhat conventional in poetry by men, but coming from a woman poet it has a special power since the woman can in fact give birth to both human life and poetry. Isis, the mother-goddess-Muse, commands, directs, protects, and infuses the growing artistic identity of the woman poet throughout the poem. The resolution is no easy one: the difficulties of being a writer are somehow part of the necessary process of writing. But as she closes the poem the voices of her critics must quiet their talk of phallic power and female insubstantiality so that they can hear the woman's voice and strength which closes H. D.'s poetic career:

> Rain falls or snow, I don't know,
> only I must stumble along, grope along,
> find my way; but believe me,
>
> I have much to sustain me.
> (*Hermetic Definition*)

Once again, however, the central issue at stake is not the mistaken theories of individual critics. What the chasm between H. D.'s poetry and the readings of some of her critics demonstrates is how distortions in this one case are part of a more general pattern in criticism by which the work of women writers is misread. Let no one argue at this point that as long as all reading is subjective one person's theories are as valid as another's. It must be recognized that distortions of a literary work which result from prejudiced political and cultural categories do have real consequences for the reputations of many writers—those of different races, nationalities, classes, and political persuasions, as well as of sex. These distortions play a central part in what literature is admitted to the informal roster of the established tradition, what literature is regularly studied and taught. Criticism is a link of the broad cultural chain that in this country, especially now that once excluded students are sitting in university classrooms, does not exist for a privileged elite alone. Consequently, criticism does not exist in a polite vacuum in which one person's views are as good as another's, in a gentlemanly sort of way. It can perpetuate the slow burying process that is suffered by writers whose vision and experience are somehow out of the more privileged mainstream. And with this burial comes the alienation of readers who cannot find their own experience reflected in what they study in college.

The growth of Women's Studies—like Afro-American Studies, Puerto Rican Studies, Chicano Studies, Asian Studies, Native American Studies—has been a necessary answer to the closed curriculums of the established literary tradition. There shoulc be no doubt that poems like *Hermetic Definition* and *Winter Love* can be studied in a course on women and literature. H. D. was a woman writer who faced the peculiar difficulties imposed on women writers by the society at large and the established literary tradition with its retinue of critics in particular. Although she never wrote her own *A Room of One's Own,* many of her novels and poems center around the problems of women artists and intellectuals. In addition, her heroes are always women; and as individuals in quest instead of abstract symbols, the women in her work are strikingly different from those in the poetry written by her male counterparts. What H. D. and poets like her have to say about women's experience and potential is as much a legitimate focus for a course as any thematic or chronological breakdown in a college curriculum. If literature and politics of the thirties, or frontier literature, or the angry young men in Britain, or the absurd in modern fiction, are all valid subjects for study, then surely women and literature must also be.

But having separate courses on women and literature is not enough; in fact this kind of separation by itself fosters the continuation of the idea that there are poets and then women poets, artists and then black artists, literature and then radical propaganda. To say that "lost" literatures by women, blacks, and other minority groups belong in separate niches all to themselves is to claim a kind of universality for literature by white males that it does not have. The poetry of H. D., along with that of other women and minority writers, should be as much a part of the training of a graduate student in modern poetry as the work of Eliot, Yeats, Williams, Crane, Stevens, Pound, and any other of the numerous male poets whose works are required reading in the universities. H. D. is a part of modern poetry—that she was a woman writing about women should not exclude her from "The Literary Tradition." What she has to say about women and men in her poetry should be as much a part of any class as what Pound or Eliot have to say about men and women. If the elite of acceptable literature will have explored the experience of only half the human race (at best), with this incompleteness, this subjectivity, it will have lost a profound understanding of its own humanity. For when men see women in terms of stereotypes, they also understand themselves inadequately.

SUSAN GUBAR

The Echoing Spell of H. D.'s Trilogy

In a wonderful children's story called *The Hedgehog,* H. D. focuses on a little girl called "Madge" or "Madgelet" whose name "isn't a name at all" and whose nationality is both English and American, although "You would think she was French too, or Swiss, when you heard her speak." Understandably, she is termed "Madd" by the natives of Leytaux who find it difficult to pronounce her name or understand her language. She, too, has problems understanding them; indeed, her quest in the story is an attempt to discover the meaning of the word *hérisson.* A wild little girl in flight from the rules and regulations of the adult world, such as the demand that she wear horrid thick boots outdoors in the garden, Madge is at the point in her life when she begins to experience self-consciousness. She is fleetingly but frighteningly aware of her separateness from the rest of creation, and it seems fitting that she is searching for an animal whose body provides a kind of natural fortress—armored protection against the slings and arrows of misfortune. This little girl's confusion at the meaning of cultural signs and her identification with the natural world recall a number of wild romantic children who are first lost and then found, but her story—which was, appropriately, written by H. D. for her daughter, Perdita—is a paradigm of a uniquely female quest for maturation that would also concern H. D. in her most ambitious poetic narratives.

Madge learns the secret meaning of the word *hérisson* only after she

From *Contemporary Literature* 19, no. 2 (Spring 1978). © 1978 by the Board of Regents of the University of Wisconsin System.

finds an educated man who owns and interprets for her a book on classical
lore that explains how *hérissons* were used by the warriors of Mycenae to
make caps and by the Athenians for combing wool. Madge's dependency on
Dr. Blum recalls not only H. D.'s subsequent reliance on Dr. Freud, but also
her mystification as a child when she "could . . . scarcely distinguish the
shape of a number from a letter, or know which was which" on the pages
of writing she saw on her father's desk. Sure, then, that her father possessed
"sacred symbols," H. D. was conscious ever after that mythic, scientific, and
linguistic symbols are controlled and defined by men. She repeatedly describes her alienation from a puzzling system of inherited symbols which do,
nevertheless, finally reveal a special meaning to the female initiate. For Madge,
the classical references and the successful completion of her quest lead to a
joyously personal experience of her own powers which she articulates in her
subsequent hymn to the moon, Artemis, who "loved girls, little girls and big
girls, and all girls who were wild and free in the mountains, and girls who
ran races just like boys along the seashore."

What undercuts the traditional Freudian interpretation of this tale as a
little girl's search for the phallus she presumably lacks is precisely this vision
of Artemis, embodying Madge's distinctively female joy and her sense that
she contains multitudes, that she exists in both the mythic past and the
secular present. Far from seeking so-called "masculine" forms of power,
Madge manages to create out of the enigmatic, recalcitrant signs of her
culture a new and sustaining story of female freedom. In her fascination with
ambiguous signs and stories with "double sorts of meaning," Madge resembles her creator, whose initials stand not only for Hilda Doolittle but also
for the *Hermetic Definitions* that would intrigue her with secret meanings
made accessible only to those who experience either themselves or their culture as alien. One of H. D.'s most coherent and ambitious poetic narratives,
her war *Trilogy,* explores the reasons for her lifelong fascination with the
palimpsest. Like Madge, H. D. presents herself as an outsider who must
express her views from a consciously female perspective, telling the truth, as
[Emily] Dickinson would say, "slant." Inheriting uncomfortable male-defined
images of women and of history, H. D. responds with palimpsestic or encoded revisions of male myths. Thus, like Madge, she discovers behind the
recalcitrant and threatening signs of her times a hidden meaning that sustains
her quest by furnishing stories of female strength and survival. In the *Trilogy,*
through recurrent references to secret languages, codes, dialects, hieroglyphs,
foreign idioms, fossilized traces, mysterious signs, and indecipherable signets,
H. D. illustrates how patriarchal culture can be subverted by the woman

who dares to "re-invoke, re-create" what has been "scattered in the shards / men tread upon."

While there is never any question for H. D. that she can avoid re-invoking or re-creating, such a posture implies that she never expects to find or make a language of her own. It is significant, I think, that H. D. sees in her famous vision at Corfu a tripod, symbol of "prophetic utterance or occult or hidden knowledge; the Priestess or Pythoness of Delphi sat on the tripod while she pronounced her verse couplets, the famous Delphic utterances which it was said *could be read two ways*" [italics mine]. Throughout her career, H. D. wrote couplets which have been read only one way. Placed in exclusively male contexts, the poetry of Freud's analysand, Pound's girlfriend, and D. H. Lawrence's Isis has been viewed from the monolithic perspective of the twentieth-century trinity of psychoanalysis, imagism, and modernism. While none of these contexts can be discounted, each is profoundly affected by H. D.'s sense of herself as a woman writing about female confinement, specifically the woman writer's struggle against entrapment within male literary conventions. Furthermore, the fact that H. D. wrote her verse so it could be read two ways demonstrates her ambivalence over self-expression: she hides her private meaning behind public words in a juggling act that tells us a great deal about the anxieties of many women poets. Reticence and resistance characterize H. D.'s revisions in the *Trilogy*, where we can trace her contradictory attitudes toward communication: in *The Walls Do Not Fall*, H. D. demonstrates the need for imagistic and lexical redefinition, an activity closely associated with the recovery of female myths, specifically the story of Isis; in *Tribute to the Angels,* she actually begins transforming certain words, even as she revises apocalyptic myth; finally, H. D. translates the story of the New Testament in *The Flowering of the Rod,* feminizing a male mythology as she celebrates the female or "feminine" Word made flesh.

Written in three parts of forty-three poems each, primarily in unrhymed couplets, H. D.'s *Trilogy* was completed between 1944 and 1946, and it deals initially with the meaning of World War II. The title of the first volume, *The Walls Do Not Fall* [hereafter referred to as *WDNF*], reveals the primacy of spatial imagery in H. D.'s analysis of a splintered world where "there are no doors" and "the fallen roof / leaves the sealed room / open to the air" (*WDNF* 1). All of civilized history has failed to create forms that can protect or nurture the inhabitants of this wasteland, and the "Apocryphal fire" threatens even the skeleton which has incomprehensibly survived. The poet is especially vulnerable in a world that worships coercion, for the sword takes precedence over the word. Such so-called "non-utilitarian" efforts as poetry are deemed irrelevant as books are burned, and the poet who identifies herself as a member of a fellowship of "nameless initiates, / born of one mother" (WDNF 13) realizes that only a shift in perspective can redeem this landscape of pain: then the fallen roofs, absent doors, and crumbling walls will be, paradoxically, transformed from houses into shrines. Furthermore, because "gods always face two-ways" (WDNF 2), H. D. considers the possibility of scratching out "indelible ink of the palimpsest" to get back to an earlier script on the still-standing walls. However, she knows that her search for "the true-rune, the right-spell" will be castigated as "retrogressive" (WDNF 2). In a world dominated by a God who demands "*Thou shall have none other gods but me*" (WDNF 37), the entire culture castigates the beauty of "Isis, Aset or Astarte" as the snare of "a harlot" (WDNF 2). But from the beginning, H. D. senses that the jealousy of this monotheistic God actually affirms the reality of those "old fleshpots" (WDNF 2). Therefore she seeks "to recover old values," although her attempt will be labeled heretical and her rhythm will be identified with "the devil's hymn" (WDNF 2).

It is only in the context of her psychological and physical dispossession that H. D.'s famous poem about the spell of the seashell can be fully understood. In her first attempt to "recover the Sceptre, / the rod of power" associated with the healing powers of Caduceus (WDNF 3), H. D. portrays herself in the image of the "mastermason" or "craftsman" mollusk within the seashell (WDNF 4). No less an emblem of defensive survival in a hostile world than the hedgehog, the mollusk opens its house / shell to the infinite sea "at stated intervals: // prompted by hunger." But, sensing its limits, it "snap[s] shut // at invasion of the limitless" in order to preserve its own existence. Managing to eat without being eaten, the mollusk serves as an object lesson when the poet advises herself and her readers to "be firm in your own small, static, limited // orbit" so that "living within, / you beget, self-out-of-self, // selfless, / that pearl-of-great-price." Self-sufficient, brave, efficient, productive, equipped to endure in a dangerous world, H. D.'s mollusk recalls Marianne Moore's snail whose "Contractility is a virtue / as modesty is a virtue," and Denise Levertov's "Snail" whose shell is both a burden and a grace. Hidden and therefore safe, the mollusk is protected in precisely the way the poet craves asylum: neither fully alive nor fully dead, half in and half out, the mollusk in its shell becomes for H. D. a tantalizing image of the self or soul safely ensconced within the person or body, always and anywhere at home.

But the fascination goes much further because the "flabby, amorphous" mollusk not only protects itself with such impenetrable material as "bone, stone, marble" but also transforms living substance into formal object, and thereby mysteriously creates the beautiful circular patterns of its house and also the perfectly spherical pearl. Shells are associated traditionally with art because the shell is a musical instrument expressing the rhythm of the waves, and H. D. would know that it was Hermes who scooped out the shell of a tortoise, converting it into a lyre which he gave, under duress, to his brother Apollo. Hermes, who later in the *Trilogy* becomes associated with alchemy, reminds us of the transformative power that creates art out of natural objects and that caused the shell to become an important dream symbol for Words-worth, who hears through it

> A loud prophetic blast of harmony;
> An Ode, in passion uttered, which foretold
> Destruction to the children of the earth
> By deluge, now at hand.
>
> *(The Prelude)*

Created within the watery world that threatens to overwhelm all of civili-zation, Wordsworth's shell warns of a return to the beginning in a flood that will cleanse and baptize the earth. H. D.'s shell also forecasts apoca-lypse; however, she characteristically emphasizes not the onrushing deluge but the paradoxical powerlessness of the infinite waves which cannot break the closed-in "egg in egg-shell."

The self-enclosed, nonreferential completeness of pearl and shell recalls H. D.'s own earlier imagistic poems, but the limits of imagism are what emerge most emphatically since the mollusk can only combat the hostile powers of the sea by snapping shut "shell-jaws." As Gaston Bachelard so brilliantly puts it [in *The Poetics of Space*], while "the animal in its box is sure of its secrets, it has become a monster of impenetrable physiognomy." H. D. has spoken of the power of her verse to "snap-shut neatly," and the analogy implies that these tidy, enclosed poems may be unable to commu-nicate or unwilling even to admit a content. Imprisoned within what amounts to a beautiful but inescapable tomb of form, the mollusk will not be cracked open or digested, but instead remains "small, static, limited," just as H. D.'s early poems refuse any interaction with the external world when they repro-duce images that seem shaped by a poet rigidly and self-consciously in con-trol of herself and her material. Far from representing the ultimate statement of her poetics, the seashell poem is a very limited statement, altered and superseded by transformations of this image as the *Trilogy* progresses.

While H. D. discusses her craft in terms of the crafts*man* mollusk, clearly she was drawn to the shell and pearl because of their feminine evocations. Associated iconographically with Venus and the Virgin, the shell is also said to represent the female genitals. It may represent pregnancy, since the pearl is a kind of seed in the womb of the shellfish, or a hope of rebirth, as in the traditionally termed "resurrection shells." This association is supported by the mythic story that Hermes created the lyre from the shell on the very day of his birth, as well as the occasional identification of the seashell with the eggshell. H. D. was careful to elaborate on these aspects of her initial self-portrait in succeeding images of female artistry. But as the poet progresses in her identification with overtly feminine forms of creation, shells become associated with "beautiful yet static, empty // old thought, old convention" (WDNF 17) as she draws her old self around her like a "dead shell" (WDNF 14). She wants not a shell into which she can withdraw but, on the contrary, an escape from entrapment: "my heart-shell // breaks open" (WDNF 25), she proclaims ecstatically when a grain, instead of a pearl, falls into the "urn" of her heart so that "the heart's alabaster / is broken" (WDNF 29). The locked-in image of female sexuality and creativity provided by male culture, complete with its emphasis on purity and impenetrability, is finally a "jar too circumscribed" (WDNF 31), and the poet renounces "fixed indigestible matter / such as shell, pearl, imagery // done to death" (WDNF 32) in her attempt to forge more liberating and nourishing images of survival.

In her next attempt to recover the scepter of power that is Caduceus, H. D. wittily decides not to become the rod itself, which is transformed into an innocent blade of grass, but the snake/worm which travels up the rod in a circuitous spiral toward heaven. Small, parasitic, and persistent, the worm can literally eat its way out of every calamity and sustain life even in the overwhelmingly large world that is its home. Although people cry out in disgust at the worm, it is "unrepentant" as it spins its "shroud," sure in its knowledge of "how the Lord God / is about to manifest" (WDNF 6). The enclosing shroud of the worm is a shell that testifies to its divinity since it adumbrates regeneration: the winged headdress, we are told, is a sign in both the snake and the emerging butterfly of magical powers of transformation, specifically of the mystery of death and rebirth experienced by all those who have endured the worm cycle to be raised into a new, higher form. Wrapped in the "shroud" of her own self (WDNF 13), the poet feels that she is a part of a poetic race who "know each other / by secret symbols" (WDNF 13) of their twice-born experience. Crawling up an "individual grass-blade / toward our individual star" (WDNF 14), these survivors are "the keepers of the secret / the carriers, the spinners // of the rare intangible thread / that binds all humanity // to ancient wisdom, / to antiquity" (WDNF 15).

It is significant that Denise Levertov centers her discussion of H. D.'s poetry on this sequence of worm poems, voicing her appreciation for poetry which provides "doors, ways in, tunnels through." When Levertov explains that H. D. "showed us a way to penetrate mystery . . . *to enter into* darkness, mystery, so that it is experienced," by darkness she means "not evil but the other side, the Hiddenness before which *man must shed his arrogance*" (Levertov [italics mine]). In Levertov's poetry, woman is described as "a shadow / . . . drawn out / on a thread of wonder," and this "thread of wonder" links woman to "the worm artist," who tills the soil and thereby pays homage to "earth, aerates / the ground of his living." Levertov makes explicit the relationship between woman and worm artist when she describes one of the "signs" under which she has been living and writing—a "Minoan Snake Goddess" who muses as she stands between two worlds, a symbol of female wisdom and regeneration.

Of course, women from the Fates to Madame Defarge have traditionally been associated with the spinning of fate, the weaving of webs, the ensnaring of men with serpentine allies or embodiments. But H. D. and Levertov reinvent the Lamia-Eve, testimony to modern defilement of Isis, in the innocuous form of the lowly worm who recalls the speaker of Psalm 22: after crying out, "I am a worm and no man; a reproach of men, and despised of the people," the petitioner in the Psalms asks that the God "who took me out of the womb" provide a loving substitute for that loss. Both H. D. and Levertov emphasize the ways in which the worm, like the woman, has been despised by a culture that cannot stop to appreciate an artistry based not on elucidation or appropriation but on homage and wonder at the hidden darkness, the mystery. Both emphasize the worm's ability to provide another womb for its own death and resurrection. With visionary realism, both insist that the only paradise worth seeing exists not behind or beyond but within the dust. While "the keepers of the secret, / the carriers, the spinners" of such "Earth Psalms" are surely men as well as women, they are all associated with traditionally female arts of weaving, with uniquely female powers of reproducing life, and with a pre-Christian tradition that embraces gods (like Ra, Osiris, Amen) who are "not at all like Jehovah" (*WDNF* 16).

The "other side, the Hiddenness" which H. D. and Levertov seek to penetrate consists precisely of those experiences unique to women which have been denied a place in our publicly acknowledged culture, specifically the experiences of female sexuality and motherhood. Told that they embody mystery to men, even if they are indifferent to their bodies' miraculous ability to hide, foster, and emit another life, women may very well experience their own concealed sex organs as curiously mysterious, separate from their consciousness. Furthermore, the abrupt and total biological shifts that distinguish female growth from the more continuous development of men is surely one reason why the worm cycle has always fascinated women. In describing the fears of growing girls, Simone de Beauvoir says, "I have known little girls whom the sight of a chrysalis plunged into a frightened reverie" [*The Second Sex*].

Confronting approving images of women that are equally degrading because they trivialize, Emily Dickinson redefines the ornamental butterfly by describing its potential for flight. She experiences confinement as her "Cocoon tightens," realizing that "A dim capacity for Wings / Demeans the Dress" she wears. We see the same conflict portrayed in Judy Chicago's recent portraits of creative women in which what she calls the "butterfly-vagina" struggles in its desire for "easy sweeps of Sky" against the enclosing geometrical boxes and scripts that attempt to contain it in the center of the canvas. Dickinson articulates this sense of contradiction:

> So I must baffle at the Hint
> And cipher at the Sign
> And make much blunder, if at last
> I take the clue divine.

The need for self-transformation creates a dilemma for Dickinson not dissimilar to H. D.'s confusion when she feels ready "to begin a new spiral" (*WDNF* 21) but finds herself thrown back on outworn vocabularies and the terrible feeling that she has failed to achieve metamorphosis. Like Dickinson, who "must baffle at the Hint," H. D. blunders over an "indecipherable palimpsest" (*WDNF* 31) which she cannot read. Floundering, "lost in sea-depth / . . . where Fish / move two-ways" (*WDNF* 30), overwhelmed by confusion at her own "pitiful reticence, // boasting, intrusion of strained / inappropriate allusion" (*WDNF* 31), H. D. admits the failure of her own invocations.

Perhaps she has failed because she has tried to evoke Ra, Osiris, Amen, Christ, God, All-father and the Holy Ghost, all the while knowing that she is an "initiate of the secret wisdom, / bride of the kingdom" (*WDNF* 31). The "illusion of lost-gods, daemons" has brought, instead of revelation, the "reversion of old values" (*WDNF* 31) which inhibits, denying as it does the validity of her female perspective. Specifically, she recalls now that the spinners who keep the secret that links humanity to the ancient wisdom are aspects of the female goddess, Isis. She must remain true to her own perspective—"the angle of incidence / equals the angle of reflection" (*WDNF* 32)—and to her own needs and hungers, so she now entreats a new energy:

"Hest, // Aset, Isis, the great enchantress, / in her attribute to Serqet, // the original great-mother, / who drove // harnessed scorpions / before her" (*WDNF* 34).

Seeking the "one-truth," to become as wise as "scorpions, *as serpents*" (*WDNF* 35), H. D. can now read her own personal psychic map to find the external realities. Specifically, she can now reevaluate "our secret hoard" (*WDNF* 36). The stars toward which the worm moves in its slow spiral toward the sky are also "little jars . . . boxes, very precious to hold further // unguent, myrrh, incense" (*WDNF* 24). They contain a promise of revelation not very different from shells and cocoons, which can also disclose secret treasures. Modern words, too, may reveal hidden meanings, thereby relinquishing their alien impenetrability, if the poet can somehow perceive their coded, palimpsestic status. Fairly early in the *Trilogy*, H. D. manages to take some small comfort in the bitter joke wrapped in the pun *cartouche:* for her contemporaries, it might mean a gun cartridge with a paper case, but she knows that it once signified the oblong figure in an Egyptian monument enclosing a sovereign's name (*WDNF* 9). This kind of irony offers potential consolation when the poet realizes that it might still be possible to disentangle ancient meanings from corrupt forms, for instance the "Christos-image . . . from its art-craft junk-shop / paint-and-plaster medieval jumble // of pain-worship and death-symbol" (*WDNF* 18). Finally the poet knows and feels

> the meaning that words hide;
>
> they are anagrams, cryptograms,
> little boxes, conditioned
>
> *to hatch butterflies.*
> (*WDNF* 39; italics mine)

H. D. learns how to decipher what that other H. D.—Humpty Dumpty—called "portmanteaus," words which open up like a bag or a book into compartments. By means of lexical reconstruction, she begins to see the possibility of purging language of its destructive associations and arbitrariness. Viewing each word as a puzzle ready to be solved and thereby freed not only of modernity but also of contingency, H. D. begins to hope that she can discover secret, coded messages. Surely these must be subversive to warrant their being so cunningly concealed by her culture.

Now *The Walls Do Not Fall* can end in a hymn to Osiris because the poet has managed to "recover the secret of Isis" (*WDNF* 40). Just as H. D. is sure that the destructive signs surrounding her can be redefined for her

own renewal, in the ancient myth Isis gathers together the scattered fragments of her lost brother/husband's body and reconstructs him in a happier
ending than that to be enacted by the King's men for Humpty Dumpty. The
resurrection of Osiris and the reconstruction of the magical power of the
Word testify to the healing, even vivifying powers of the poet-Isis who can
now see the unity between Osiris and Sirius. Since Sirius is the star representing Isis come to wake her brother from death, such an equation means
that the poet glimpses the shared identity of the sibling lovers Osiris and
Isis. Approaching this "serious" mystery, H. D. asks, "O, Sire, is" this union
between the god and the goddess finally possible (WDNF 42)? She can even
connect "Osiris" with the "zrr-hiss" of war-lightning. The poet who uses
words with reverence can release the coded messages contained or enfolded
within them. She has found the "alchemist's key" which "unlocks secret
doors" (WDNF 30). Although the walls still do not fall, continuing to testify
to the divisions and barriers between people, between historical periods,
within consciousness itself, they also preserve remnants of written messages—anagrams and cryptograms—which, by providing the link from the
present back to the past, allow H. D. to evade the destructive definitions of
reality provided by those who utilize the word for modern mastery.

The poet's response in the subsequent volumes of the Trilogy to the
shattered fragmentation of her world is stated in the first poem of Tribute
to the Angels: dedicating herself to Hermes Trismegistus, patron of alchemists, H. D. undertakes not merely the archeological reconstruction of a lost
past, but also a magical transfiguration not unlike Christ's creation of the
sustaining loaves and fishes or the transubstantiation of bread and water into
body and blood. Since alchemical art has traditionally been associated with
fiery purification that resurrects what is decomposing in the grave into a
divine and golden form, even the destructive lightning and bombs can now
be associated with melting that fuses a new unity, heat that transforms the
contents of the dross in the alchemist's bowl into the philosopher's stone.
The seashell of The Walls Do Not Fall becomes a testimony to such displacement, reappearing as a bowl which is cauldron, grave, and oven, yet another
womb in which a new jewel can be created. Now the poet sees the function
of the poem/bowl as the transformative redefinition of language itself. Thus
she gives us the recipe by which she endows "a word most bitter, marah"
and a word denigrated, "Venus," with more affirmative nurturing meanings:
"marah" becomes "Mother" and "Venus" is translated from "venery" to
"venerate" (Tribute to the Angels; hereafter referred to as TA, 8, 12). Similarly, she seeks a way of evading names that definitely label the word-jewel
in the bowl: "I do not want to name it," she explains, because "I want to

minimize thought, // concentrate on it / till I shrink, // dematerialize / and am drawn into it" (*TA* 14). Seeking a noncoercive vocabulary, a new language that will consecrate what has been desecrated by her culture, H. D. tries to re-establish the primacy of what masculine culture has relegated to a secondary place as "feminine."

Implicitly heretical, Hermes' alchemy is associated with "candle and script and bell," with "what the new-church spat upon" (*TA* 1), and H. D. does not evade the challenge her own alchemical art constitutes to the prevailing Christian conception of the Word. On the contrary, in *Tribute to the Angels* she self-consciously sets her narrative in the context of the Book of Revelation, quoting directly from it in numerous poems in order to question John's version of redemption while offering her own revision. In many poems she seems to be arguing with John directly because his vision appears warped: H. D. quotes John's assertion of the finality of his own account, his admonition that *"if any man shall add // God shall add unto him the plagues,"* even as she determines to alter his story, dedicating herself to making all things new (*TA* 3). She realizes that "he of the seventy-times-seven / passionate, bitter wrongs" is also "he of the seventy-times-seven / bitter, unending wars" (*TA* 3), and she questions the severity and punishing cruelty of John's apocalypse, with its vengeful version of the hidden future. While John sings the praises of seven angels whose seven golden bowls pour out the wrath of God upon the earth, H. D. calls on seven angels whose presence in war-torn London is a testament to the promise of rebirth that her bowl holds. While "*I John saw*" a series of monstrosities and disasters on the face of the earth, H. D. claims that "my eyes saw" a sign of resurrection; "a half-burnt-out apple-tree / blossoming" (*TA* 23) is the fulfillment of her hopes at the beginning of the *Trilogy* to recover the scepter, the lily-bud rod of Caduceus, which is now associated with the Tree of Life that links heaven and earth, the Cosmic Tree which represents the mysterious but perpetual regeneration of the natural world, the tree that miraculously lodges the coffin of the dead Osiris or the tree on which Christ was hung to be reborn. Aaron's rod which made the bitter (marah) waters sweet when it blossomed in the desert for the wandering children of Israel is converted from a sign of Moses' control to an emblem of a Lady's presence.

Most significantly, H. D. contrasts the final vision of the holy Jerusalem—a city with no need of the sun or the moon because lit by the glory of God, a city which John imagines as the bride of the Lamb—with her own final revelation of redemption. H. D. first describes a Lady in a bedroom lit by the "luminous disc" of the clock by her bedhead, ironically commenting that this room has "no need / of the moon to shine in it" (*TA* 25). But this

appearance is only a dream adumbration of the vision of this same Lady
who appears when H. D. is "thinking of Gabriel / of the moon-cycle, of the
moon-shell, // of the moon-crescent / and the moon at full" (*TA* 28). Far
from seeking a place with no need of moonshine, H. D. celebrates a Lady
who is actually the representative of lunar time and consciousness. Furthermore, the poet is careful to remind us through a whole series of negatives
that this Lady, whom we recognize from the various portraits of the female
as she has been worshipped by various cultures, is like none of these previous
representatives or incarnations. "None of these / suggest her" as the poet
sees her (*TA* 31). H. D.'s vision of the Lady is not hieratic or frozen: "she
is no symbolic figure." While she has "the dove's symbolic purity," and
"veils / like the Lamb's Bride," H. D. is insistent that "the Lamb was not
with her / either as Bridegroom or Child"; not He, but "*we* are her bridegroom and lamb" (*TA* 39; italics mine).

The miraculous transformation in the alchemical bowl and the equally
mysterious flowering of the rod find their culmination in this revelation of
the muse who is not only the veiled goddess, Persephone, the *Sanctus Spiritus,
Santa Sophia,* Venus, Isis, and Mary, but most importantly the female spirit
liberated from precisely these mystifications:

> but she is not shut up in a cave
> like Sibyl; she is not
>
> imprisoned in leaden bars
> in a coloured window;
>
> she is Psyche, *the butterfly,
> out of the cocoon.*
> (*TA* 38; italics mine)

Unnamed and elusive, the Lady recalls in her flight the hatched and winged
words of H. D. herself, if only because this visionary Lady carries a book
which "is our book" (*TA* 39). Whether this "tome of the ancient wisdom"
whose pages "are the blank pages / of the unwritten volume of the new" (*TA*
38) is "a tribute to the Angels" (*TA* 41) or a "tale of a jar or jars" (*TA* 39)
that will constitute the next volume of the *Trilogy,* H. D. closely identifies
this new Eve who has come to retrieve what was lost at the apple tree with
her own liberating revisions of the past. Whatever volume of the poem she
may carry or inspire, the Lady reflects H. D.'s hope that her narrative is a
"Book of Life" (*TA* 36).

As she evokes and thereby reinterprets the inherited signs of her culture
which are said to contain the secret wisdom necessary for the attainment of

paradise, H. D. implies that "the letter killeth but the spirit giveth life" (2 Cor. 3:6). It is life that she sees finally created in the crucible "when the jewel / melts" and what we find is "a cluster of garden-pinks / or a face like a Christmas-rose" (*TA* 43). In the final book of the *Trilogy*, the escaping fragrance of such flowering within the pristine glass of a jar represents the poet's success in finding a form that can contain without confining. No longer surrounded by splintered shards, H. D. makes of her jars symbols of aesthetic shape not unlike those of Wallace Stevens or Hart Crane, beautiful and complete objects but also transparencies through which a healing content is made manifest. Purified of their opacity, shell, bowl, and box are now ready to reveal their previously secret and therefore inaccessible hoard. This promise of release is realized fully in *The Flowering of the Rod* [hereafter referred to as *FR*]: dedicated to the Lady who has escaped conventionally defined categories, the poet readies herself for flight as she asks us to "leave the smouldering cities below" (*FR* 1), the place of deathly skulls, to follow the quest of Christ, who was "the first to wing / from that sad Tree" (*FR* 11) and whose journey is similar to that of the snow-geese circling the Arctic or the mythical migratory flocks seeking paradise.

Not only does H. D. move further back in time in this third volume of the *Trilogy*, but her initial focus on seemingly insignificant animals and her subsequent naming of angelic powers seem to have made it possible for her to finally create human characters as she retells the story of the birth and death of Christ from the unexpected perspective of two participants in the gospel—Kaspar the Magian and Mary Magdala. Furthermore, after two sequences of poems progressing by allusive associations, complex networks of imagery, and repetitive, almost liturgical invocations, the final book of the *Trilogy* embodies the emergence of the poet's sustained voice in a story—if not of her own making—of her own perspective. She takes an unusual stance toward the ancient story to distinguish her vision: claiming to see "what men say is-not," to remember what men have forgot (*FR* 6), she sets out to testify to an event known by everyone but as yet unrecorded (*FR* 12).

Like Christ, who was himself "an outcast and a vagabond" (*FR* 11), and like the poet who is identified with the thief crucified by His side, both Kaspar and Mary are aliens in their society. The inheritor of ancient alchemical tradition, Kaspar owns the jars which hold "priceless, unobtainable-elsewhere / myrrh" (*FR* 13), a "distillation" which some said "lasted literally forever," the product of "sacred processes" which were "never written, not even in symbols" (*FR* 14). As a heathen, he represents pre-Biblical lore that acknowledges the power of "daemons" termed "devils" by the modern Christian world. His education, however, is a patrimony in an exclusively male tradition that assumes "no secret was safe with a woman" (*FR* 14). Kaspar is shown to be a bit of a prig and something of a misogynist, so it is highly incongruous that Mary Magdala comes to this Arab stranger in his "little booth of a house" (*FR* 13) behind the market. Unmaidenly and unpredictable, Mary is as much of an outcast as Kaspar, if only because of her ability "to detach herself," a strength responsible for her persistence in spite of Kaspar's statement that the myrrh is not for sale: "planted" before him (*FR* 15), Mary identifies herself first as "Mary, a great tower," and then explains that, though she is "Mara, bitter," through her own power she will be "Mary-myrrh" (*FR* 16). Clearly, the coming together of Kaspar and Mary implies the healing of the poet's own sense of fragmentation. Before the jar actually changes hands, however, H. D. dramatizes the discomfort of Simon, who views Mary at the Last Supper as a destructive siren. This "woman from the city" who seems "devil-ridden" to the Christian is recognized by Kaspar as a living embodiment of the indwelling daemons of "Isis, Astarte, Cyprus / and the other four; // he might re-name them, / Ge-meter, De-meter, earth-mother // or Venus / in a star" (*FR* 25).

Only after we have recognized the seemingly antithetical wise man and the whore as common representatives of reverence for the ancient principles of female fertility and creativity does H. D. return to the scene in the booth behind the market to fully describe the vision granted to Kaspar through the intervention of Mary. Here, at the climax of the *Trilogy*, Kaspar recalls the poet's experience with the Lady, for he is graced with a remembrance of "when he saw the light on her hair / like moonlight on a lost river" (*FR* 27). In a fleck or a flaw of a jewel on the head of one of three crowned ladies, Kaspar discovers "the whole secret of the mystery" (*FR* 30). He sees the circles of islands and the lost center island, Atlantis; he sees earth before Adam, Paradise before Eve. Finally, he hears a spell in an unknown language which seems to come down from prehistoric times as it translates itself to him:

> *Lilith born before Eve*
> *and one born before Lilith,*
> *and Eve; we three are forgiven,*
> *we are three of the seven*
> *daemons cast out of her.*
> (*The Flowering of the Rod*)

This is an extremely enigmatic message, but it does seem to imply that a matriarchal genealogy had been erased from recorded history when this ancient female trinity was exorcised as evil, cast out of human consciousness by those who would begin in the Garden with Eve. Since Lilith is a woman who dared pronounce the Ineffable Name and who was unabashed at articulating her sexual preferences, her presence among the crowned or crucified queens seems to promise a prelapsarian vision quite different from that of Genesis: Lilith, Eve, and the unnamed daemon are three of the seven who establish a link back to Kaspar's pagan daemons; together they promise a submerged but now recoverable time of female strength, female speech, and female sexuality, all of which have mysteriously managed to survive, although in radically subdued ways, incarnate in the body of Mary Magdala. As a healer, a shaman of sorts, Kaspar has in a sense recaptured Mary's stolen soul, her lost ancestors; he has established the matriarchal genealogy that confers divinity upon her.

Reading Mary like a palimpsest, Kaspar has fully penetrated the secret of the mystery. H. D. then reverses the chronology of his life, moving backward from his confrontation with this Mary over the jars of myrrh to his delivery of the gift of myrrh to the Virgin Mary. When Kaspar thinks in the ox stall that "there were always two jars" (*FR* 41) and that "*someday* [he] *will bring the other*" (*FR* 42), we know that his prophecy has been or will be fulfilled: as he gives the myrrh to the Virgin, we know that he is destined to give the other jar to Mary Magdala, thereby authenticating his vision of the female trinity—his knowledge that the whore is the mother and that Isis, who has been labeled a retrogressive harlot, is actually the regenerative goddess of life. Through the two Marys, Kaspar recovers the aspects of Isis retained by Christianity—the lady of sorrows weeping for the dead Osiris and the divine mother nursing her son, Horus. When marah is shown to be mother the translation is complete, and the poem can end with a new word, as the gift is miraculously appreciated by a Mary who might know that the blossoming, flowering fragrance is the commingling of the magical contents of the jar, the myrrh in her arms, and perhaps even the baby in her lap.

Dramatically ending at the beginning, moving from Apocalypse to Genesis, from death to birth, from history to mystery, H. D. illustrates the cyclical renewal she personally seeks of dying into life. Calling our attention to her own narrative principles, H. D. proclaims: "I have gone forward. / I have gone backward" (*FR* 8). And as we have seen, her point is precisely the need of going backward in time to recover what has been lost in the past, for this justifies her own progress backward in chronological time throughout the *Trilogy:* proceeding from the modern times of London in *The Walls Do Not Fall* to the medieval cities of *Tribute to the Angels* and back to the ancient deserts of Israel in *The Flowering of the Rod*, she dedicates herself to finding the half-erased traces of a time "When in the company of the gods / I loved and was loved" (*WDNF* 5). Such a discovery, as we have seen, involves not a learning but a remembering. However, instead of moving backward in a linear, sequential manner, she chooses three time bands that seem to be relatively self-contained, like ever-narrowing circles enclosing some still point of origin. Furthermore, she calls our attention to the disconnectedness of her three time spheres by isolating each within a book of the *Trilogy*. These three distinct periods in time, when taken in themselves, are senseless and directionless, each repeating the other:

> you think, even before it is half-over,
> that your cycle is at an end,
>
> but you repeat your foolish circling—again, again, again;
> again, the steel sharpened on the stone;
>
> again, the pyramid of skulls.
>
> (*The Flowering of the Rod*)

The senseless wheeling within each of these foolish cycles, caused by the lack of vision that cannot see "then" as an aspect of "now," is fittingly experienced as a tornado (*WDNF* 32). It can produce only war.

LOUIS L. MARTZ

Introduction to The Collected Poems

"I believe in women doing what they like," says Mrs. Carter in H. D.'s *Bid Me to Live*. "I believe in the modern woman." But then the author adds: "In 1913, the 'modern woman' had no special place on the map, and to be 'modern' in Mrs. Carter's sense, after 1914, required some very specific handling. 'I believe in intelligent women having experience' was then a very, very thin line to toe, a very, very frail wire to do a tight-rope act on." For Hilda Doolittle, born in Bethlehem, Pennsylvania, in 1886 and reared in her mother's strict Moravian tradition, the move to London in 1911 and life in the circles of Ezra Pound, Richard Aldington, and D. H. Lawrence offered her the modern experience, along that very thin line, that very frail wire.

Her situation, as it developed, became very close to the role of Astrid that she played in the movie *Borderline*, made by Kenneth Macpherson in 1930. As H. D. explains in a pamphlet that she wrote about the movie, Astrid and her lover Thorne have come to a "borderline town of some indefinite mid-European mountain district . . . because of some specific nerve-problem, perhaps to rest, perhaps to recuperate, perhaps to economise, perhaps simply in hope of some emotional convalescence. They live as such people do the world over, in just such little social borderline rooms as just such couples seek in Devonshire, in Cornwall . . ."—places that H. D. knows well. "They are borderline social cases, not out of life, not in life . . . Astrid, the white-cerebral is and is not outcast, is and is not a social alien, is and is not a normal human being, she is borderline."

From *H. D.: Collected Poems 1912–1944*, edited by Louis L. Martz. © 1983 by Louis L. Martz. New Directions Publishing Co., 1983.

Her poetry and her prose, like her own psyche, live at the seething junction of opposite forces. Whoever conceived the original jacket design for *Bid Me to Live* realized the central truth about her work; for the jacket displays the active, shifting scene where land and ocean meet. This junction is the setting for many of her earliest poems: "Sea Rose," "Sea Poppies," "Sea Violet," "Sea Gods," "Sea Iris"—these poems scattered throughout her first book, *Sea Garden* (1916), are only the most obvious examples of the basic theme of the entire volume: the "beauty" that results from the fierce clashing of natural forces, as in "Sea Poppies":

> your stalk has caught root
> among wet pebbles
> and drift flung by the sea
> and grated shells
> and split conch-shells.

She cannot abide the "Sheltered Garden":

> For this beauty,
> beauty without strength,
> chokes out life.
> I want wind to break,
> scatter these pink-stalks,
> snap off their spiced heads,
> fling them about with dead leaves
>
> . . . .
>
> O to blot out this garden
> to forget, to find a new beauty
> in some terrible
> wind-tortured place.

Even this early volume shows the inadequacy of the term "Imagist" when applied to this poet. For "Imagism" may suggest a crystalline formation, static, brief, a quick moment of apprehension, as in Pound's classic "In a Station of the Metro" or in Lawrence's "Green"—

> The dawn was apple-green,
>   The sky was green wine held up in the sun,
> The moon was a golden petal between.
>
> She opened her eyes, and green
>   They shone, clear like flowers undone
> For the first time, now for the first time seen.

But even the poems of H. D. that Pound read in 1912 will not fit so limited
a view of Imagism. "Hermes of the Ways" was one of these, and the cross-
roads that this god inhabits is again the junction of sea and shore:

> Dubious,
> facing three ways,
> welcoming wayfarers,
> he whom the sea-orchard
> shelters from the west,
> from the east
> weathers sea-wind;
> fronts the great dunes.
>
> Wind rushes
> over the dunes,
> and the coarse, salt-crusted grass
> answers.
>
> Heu,
> it whips round my ankles!

It is true that her poems in *Sea Garden* tend to meet the principles set
forth by Pound, H. D., and Aldington in 1912: she gives "direct treatment
of the 'thing' whether subjective or objective"; she tries "to use absolutely
no word that does not contribute to the presentation"—though sometimes
her exclamations overrun the mark; and as for rhythm, she certainly com-
poses "in the sequence of the musical phrase." Most of the poems too will
meet Pound's definition of the "Image" as "that which presents an intellectual and emotional complex in an instant of time," if we allow the "complex"
to hold the psychological overtones that Pound intends and if the complex
is created by the interaction of many images within an "instant" of considerable duration.

What is important is that the doctrines of Imagism provided H. D. with
a discipline that enabled her to control the surges that arose from the depths
of her violently responsive nature. William Carlos Williams gives us a
glimpse of this in his *Autobiography*, when he tells of a walk that he took
with H. D. through the countryside near her home outside Philadelphia,
where Ezra Pound and he (especially Ezra) used to visit often during their
student days. A thunderstorm arose, and Williams looked for shelter. "We
were at the brink of a grassy pasture facing west, quite in the open, and the
wind preceding the storm was in our faces. . . . Instead of running or even
walking toward a tree Hilda sat down in the grass at the edge of the hill

and let it come. 'Come, beautiful rain,' she said, holding out her arms. 'Beautiful rain, welcome.'"

Her ecstatic response to the forces of nature is characteristic: it is the union of self with nature that she creates in her famous "Oread" (1914), where the spirit of the Greek mountain-nymph comprehends the waves of the ocean as the pines of her own shore, in one dynamic and unified complex:

> Whirl up, sea—
> whirl your pointed pines,
> splash your great pines
> on our rocks,
> hurl your green over us,
> cover us with your pools of fir.

To live constantly at the juncture of such forces, inner and outer, to inhabit constantly the borderline—this was to be the life that lay ahead for H. D., as person and as poet.

For a time, as in "Oread" or "Hermes of the Ways," the combination of Imagist principles with Greek myths and themes served to focus her responses; Greek myths in particular served as dramatic masks and channels. But by 1916–17 the infidelities of Richard Aldington (whom she had married in 1913, after her close friendship with Pound had faltered) created a sense of betrayal that became too strong for these modes of mythic or poetic control. The story is told in a triad of poems, "Amaranth," "Eros," and "Envy," preserved in a carefully bound typescript containing only these poems and bearing on the flyleaf the inscription in H. D.'s hand: "Corfe Castle–Dorset–summer 1917–from poems of The Islands series–" The date should probably be 1916, for that was the summer she spent at Corfe Castle, while Richard Aldington was beginning his military training nearby. "The Islands" was published in 1920, but it is significant that H. D. could not bring herself to publish the trio of poems, in any form, until 1924, when portions of them appeared in Heliodora, dispersed among other poems, and masked as expansions of fragments of Sappho. The association with the years 1916–17, with Aldington, and with "The Islands" (a poem that evokes the legend of Ariadne) gives us the necessary clues to the trio, for these are all poems that enact the anguish of a deserted woman.

The situation within the three poems is basically the same as that presented in Bid Me to Live, where the husband of Julia (counterpart of H. D.) has flagrantly betrayed her with a woman who, in Julia's eyes, has merely physical attractions—and earlier, there was another woman. The betrayal has arisen in large part from Julia's own frigidity, caused by the death of her stillborn child and the subsequent warning of the nurse that she must not have another child until the war had ended. The speaker of "Amaranth" refers to her apparent coolness and her failure to respond:

> I was not indifferent when I strayed aside
> or loitered as we three went,
> or seemed to turn a moment from the path
> for that same amaranth.
>
> I was not dull and dead when I fell
> back on our couch at night.
> I was not indifferent though I turned
> and lay quiet.
> I was not dead in my sleep.

She makes a valiant effort toward a generous gesture, giving her praise to Aphrodite for the love that her lover bears "for his mistress":

> Let him go forth radiant,
> let life rise in his young breast,
> life is radiant,
> life is made for beautiful love
> and strange ecstasy,
> strait, searing body and limbs,
> tearing limbs and body from life;
> life is his if he ask,
> life is his if he take it,
> then let him take beauty
> as his right.

But she cannot make that gift so easily. In the final section the effort recoils upon itself and she turns to denounce her faithless lover:

> how I hate you for this,
> how I despise and hate,
> was my beauty so slight a gift,
> so soon, so soon forgot?

And then in desperation she cries out:

> Turn, for I love you yet,
> though you are not worthy my love,
> though you are not equal to it.

"Turn back," she cries again, "before death strike, / for the goddess speaks."
And what the goddess says to the man is this: the two are both poets of
Aphrodite, and they belong together:

> *Turn if you will from her path*
> *for one moment seek*
> *a lesser beauty*
> *and a lesser grace,*
> *but you will find*
> *no peace in the end*
> *save in her presence.*

The first three sections of "Amaranth" (out of five) appear in *Heliodora*
under the title "Fragment Forty-one / . . . *thou flittest to Andromeda.* / Sappho." The rest of the fragment is important: "So you hate me now, Atthis,
and / Turn towards Andromeda." For the title was not merely an after-
thought: this fragment by Sappho underlies the original version of the poem,
where, instead of the words "Aphrodite, shameless and radiant," the first
section reads: "Andromeda, shameless and radiant," while the second section
adds the other name:

> Nay, O my lover, Atthis:
> shameless and still radiant
> I tell you this.

Thus the attributes of the goddess are carried over subtly to describe the
three mortals involved. H. D. has performed a bitterly clever adaptation:
Atthis was a woman in Sappho's poetry, but the male fertility god Attis was
a counterpart of Adonis—who provided the title and theme for another poem
of these years.

The poem "Eros" follows directly from the cry "Turn back" at the close
of "Amaranth." Now the speaker calls to the love-god in agony: "Where is
he taking us / now that he has turned back?" And the "fever" of her passion
leads to the most intimate account of physical love to be found in H. D.'s
early poetry. But the passion cannot be kept: the lover is drifting away, again:

> Is it bitter to give back
> love to your lover if he wish it
> for a new favourite,
> who can say,
> or is it sweet?

Yet there is poetic compensation: "to sing love, / love must first shatter us."

In 1924 the last five sections of "Eros" (out of seven) appeared in *Heliodora* under the title "Fragment Forty / *Love . . . bitter-sweet.* / Sappho." But the first two sections were omitted; they were too personal, too intimate, for public presentation. The Greek mask had to cover the personal cry: "Once again limb-loosening Love [Eros] makes me tremble, the bitter-sweet, irresistible creature."

"Envy" is directly related to the wartime threat of death to the lover: "I envy you your chance of death, / how I envy you this."

> what can death loose in me
> after your embrace?
> your touch,
> your limbs are more terrible
> to do me hurt.
>
> What can death mar in me
> that you have not?

And in this fearful context she remembers a gentle gift of violets that he had brought to her, perhaps in that nursing home in 1915 after the death of their child—an incident recorded in her unpublished "Autobiographical Notes": "R. brings huge bunch of violets."

> You gathered violets,
> You spoke:
> "your hair is not less black
> nor less fragrant,
> nor in your eyes is less light . . ."
> why were those slight words
> and the violets you gathered
> of such worth?

But the poem ends with a death wish, conceding victory to the goddess of "Amaranth":

> crushed under the goddess' hate,
> though I fall beaten at last,
> so high have I thrust my glance
> up into her presence.
>
> Do not pity me, spare that,
> but how I envy you
> your chance of death.

In 1924 three sections out of the four appeared in *Heliodora* under the title: "Fragment Sixty-eight / ... *even in the house of Hades.* / Sappho." Again, the missing third section would have revealed too much:

> Could I have known
> you were more male than the sun-god,
> more hot, more intense,
> could I have known?
> for your glance all-enfolding,
> sympathetic, was selfless
> as a girl's glance.

In all the revisions of these poems the evidence that the faithless lover is male has been removed; for this would not belong to the mask of Sappho. And yet, if indeed the rest of this last Sappho fragment was recalled by these two poet-lovers, what a bitter sting is implied, for Sappho there denies poetic immortality to the person addressed: "But when you die you will lie there, and afterwards there will never be any recollection of you or any longing for you since you have no share in the roses of Pieria; unseen in the house of Hades also, flown from our midst, you will go to and fro among the shadowy corpses."

It is clear, from the original version of these three poems, that by 1916–17 H. D. was beginning to create a strongly personal voice, breaking out of the Imagist confines, breaking through the Greek mask. One suspects that this tendency toward greater openness was encouraged by her friendship with D. H. Lawrence, which began in 1914 and ended abruptly about 1918, after they had exchanged poems and letters for several years. We shall probably never know the whole truth about this relationship, since Lawrence's letters to H. D. were destroyed by Aldington (as part of a more general destruction of letters). But from "Advent" (the extracts from her journal of Freud's treatment), from her unpublished letters, and especially from *Bid Me to Live*, we can grasp the essentials and realize how deeply Lawrence influenced her life and poetry.

Normally, of course, it would be risky to trust a work cast in the form of a novel for autobiographical facts—and with many of H. D.'s prose writings a great deal of caution should be used, since she tended to fictionalize and fantasize. But *Bid Me to Live* constitutes a special case, for it was written under advice from Freud himself that she should write *history*. "I have been soaking in D. H. L. letters," she writes to her friend Bryher (Winifred Ellerman) on May 15, 1933, "not too good for me, but Freud seems to agree with me for once. Evidently I blocked the whole of the 'period' and if I can skeleton-in a vol. about it, it will break the clutch." She says that she has "the counters sorted out," but then she adds the crucial point: "the 'cure' will be, I fear me, writing that damn vol. straight, as history, no frills as in Narthex, Palimp., and so on, just a straight narrative, then later, changing names and so on." And again, after she has been reading Middleton Murry's book on Lawrence, *Son of Woman*, she writes to Bryher (May 18, 1933): "papa [Freud] seems to believe explicitly that it would be best for me to make this vol. of mine about 1913–1920 explicit." Freud, she says, thinks that her dreams show that a "bridge" has now been made in her unconscious, and that the whole psychoanalysis "now is more or less 'over' (in the primitive sense) but it will need a lot of 'guts,' (my word) my end, to get the thing down in a stern manner and not leap goat-like on the top of things in a dope-y stream of consciousness like Narthex."

Freud's advice, then, explains why *Bid Me to Live* has a style so different in its tautness, terseness, and directness, when compared with the "goat-like" style of some of her other prose works. The essential point to note here is that *Bid Me to Live* makes it plain that there was never any physical relationship with Lawrence. Their relationship was, I believe, very much like Lawrence's relations with half a dozen other women—spiritual, poetical, emotional, erotic in part, but not carnal: exactly as Lawrence describes it in the letter to Cecil Gray where Lawrence includes "Hilda Aldington" among his "women," as Gray has evidently called them. For Lawrence these women represent "the threshold of a new world, or underworld, of knowledge and being. . . . my 'women' want an ecstatic subtly-intellectual underworld, like the Greeks—Orphicism—like Magdalene at her feet-washing—"

Bid Me to Live also provides some glimpses of what Lawrence thought of H. D.'s poetry. Speaking of Rico (Lawrence) she writes: "You jeered at my making abstractions of people—graven images, you called them. You are right. Rafe [Aldington] is not the Marble Faun, not even a second-rate Dionysus. I wrote that cyclamen poem for him in Dorset, at Corfe Castle, where I wrote your Orpheus. But you are right. He is not Dionysus, you are not Orpheus. You are human people, Englishmen, madmen." Lawrence would have liked that outburst: it shows the kind of anger that he admired. The "cyclamen poem" is "The God" (1917), where the male lover is treated as a Dionysus descended to earth, flooding the speaker with the "cyclamen-purple" of passion: "cyclamen-red, colour of the last grapes." And yet there is a touch of foreboding, a sense that the poem is already an elegy: "I thought I would be the last / you would want . . ." "Your Orpheus" is apparently the poem "Eurydice" (1917), though its published form may not be the original version. Here the female speaker bitterly laments the backward glance of the

Orpheus-figure who, "for your arrogance / and your ruthlessness," has defeated her return to the flowers and the light of the upper world toward
which he seemed to be leading her. Now through his failure she is condemned
to this place "where dead lichens drip / dead cinders upon moss of ash."
Nevertheless at the close she accepts her plight with a firm reliance upon her
inward strength:

> At least I have the flowers of myself,
> and my thoughts, no god
> can take that;
> I have the fervour of myself for a presence
> and my own spirit for light.

Still, if we trust *Bid Me to Live,* she has not yet grasped what Lawrence
has been trying to tell her:

> He had written about love, about her frozen altars: "Kick over
> your tiresome house of life," he had said, he had jeered, "frozen
> lily of virtue," he had said, "our languid lily of virtue nods per-
> ilously near the pit," he had written, "come away where the angels
> come down to earth"; "crucible" he had called her, "burning
> slightly blue of flame"; "love-adept" he had written, "you are a
> living spirit in a living spirit city."

"What did he mean?" she asks. What sort of invitation is implied? But the
pre-Raphaelite imagery, with the allusion to Rossetti's "House of Life,"
seems to indicate that he is talking mainly about her poetry, about the attitudes toward life in her poetry: it is frozen, dividing the spirit from the
earth. He seems to be urging her to strike out on her own, be free and
human, as he himself was attempting to be in his own poetry at this time:
the poems of *Look! We Have Come Through!*—of which, Lawrence reports,
"Hilda Aldington says they won't do at all: they are not *eternal,* not subli-
mated: too much body and emotions."

But in 1918, or thereabouts, after she had gone off with Cecil Gray to
Cornwall, the friendship ended. Rico-Lawrence had warned her: "Do you
realize," he said, "what you are doing?" [*Bid Me to Live*]. What she was
doing was breaking the image, shattering the role that Lawrence had conceived for her: the disciple, the believer, the Tree of Life that she played for
Lawrence in that charade of *Bid Me to Live.* All this she was destroying. " 'I
hope never to see you again,' he wrote in that last letter," she records in
"Advent." The effect was disastrous: Pound, Aldington, Lawrence—all her
best-loved men had left her.

Then Bryher saved her, in the depths of illness and despair, after the birth of her daughter in the spring of 1919; and the voyage to Greece in 1920 brought back her health and her poetry—but with another tension and still under the masks of Greece. That painfully open poem, "I Said," written in the winter of 1919 and dedicated to "W.B.," remained unpublished until 1982, while the borderline problems of her psyche reveal themselves guardedly in the volume *Hymen* (1921). Here the opening masque of "Hymen" seems to celebrate a bridal of the past, with manifold allusions to music that suggest a relation with someone deeply musical—and Cecil Gray was a composer. Then in the same volume we find the poem headed "Not Honey"— later given the full title: "Fragment One Hundred Thirteen / *"Neither honey nor bee for me."* / Sappho."—where the speaker with reluctant memory seems to renounce male love and accept the Sapphic lyre. It is the same ambivalence that marks the much more painful "Fragment Thirty-six / *I know not what to do: / my mind is divided.* / Sappho," published in *Poetry* in 1921, where the state of mind is expressed in her favorite imagery of the wave-crest:

> I know not what to do:
> strain upon strain,
> sound surging upon sound
> makes my brain blind;
> as a wave-line may wait to fall
> yet (waiting for its falling)
> still the wind may take
> from off its crest,
> white flake on flake of foam,
> that rises,
> seeming to dart and pulse
> and rend the light,
> so my mind hesitates
> above the passion
> quivering yet to break,
> so my mind hesitates
> above my mind,
> listening to song's delight.

Here is the deep center of her poetry, but it can only be dealt with through a mask; it cannot be directly explored, as it was in "Amaranth." Here is the borderline state: between old values and new, between old loves and new, between physical passion and poetical dedication.

The result, for a time, is fine poetry. But the strain was too great. She could not find the confidence to open out, as Lawrence had urged. *Heliodora* (1924) is a good volume, but much of it derives from the previous decade, as far back as 1913. Now, in the later 1920s, she tries many modes of writing: the three-act verse drama *Hippolytus Temporizes* (1927), successful only in its lyric parts; prose fiction; translations from the Greek. But her volume of 1931, *Red Roses for Bronze,* shows no development: the Greek mask is still holding, even more tightly, and, despite some excellent sequences (such as "Let Zeus Record") the struggle for expression is almost desperate in places, as in the tendency to heap up repetitions that cry out after emotion, but do not create it:

> I live,
> I live,
> I live,
> you give me that;
> this gift of ecstasy
> is rarer,
> dearer
> than any monstrous pearl
> from tropic water;
> I live,
> I live,
> I live.

This is pitiful, grasping for a response the words cannot command. H. D. seems to realize that she has come to the end of a road, and so, near the close of this volume, she places her "Epitaph":

> So I may say,
> "I died of living,
> having lived one hour";
>
> so they may say,
> "she died soliciting
> illicit fervour";
>
> so you may say,
> "Greek flower; Greek ecstasy
> reclaims for ever

> one who died
> following
> intricate songs' lost measure."

Realizing her condition, H. D. sought psychiatric help, first in London, and then in Vienna, where she consulted with Freud himself for three months in 1933 and for five weeks in 1934. The story of that treatment and its success is best told by H. D. herself in the two parts of her *Tribute to Freud*— in many ways the best introduction to H. D.'s life and writings that we possess. Here all one needs to say is that Freud restored her confidence in herself as a gifted woman and renewed the ability to create a personal voice that she had begun to develop in "Amaranth," "Eros," and "Envy," so many years before. . . .

"The Master" reveals, with an intimacy and anguish beyond anything in her prose *Tribute,* how Freud taught her to accept and understand the ambivalent responses of her nature as a part of God's creation:

> I did not know how to differentiate
> between volcanic desire,
> anemones like embers
> and purple fire
> of violets
> like red heat,
> and the cold
> silver
> of her feet:
>
> I had two loves separate;
> God who loves all mountains,
> alone knew why
> and understood
> and told the old man
> to explain
>
> the impossible,
>
> which he did.

But she had trouble in grasping what he taught, for she was made intensely angry by "his talk of the man-strength," and by his apparently casual and inadequate explanation, "You are a poet." Gradually, the implication is, she came to realize that to have "two loves separate" was the lot of many a creative artist (one thinks of Lawrence and of Shakespeare, in the Sonnets). "You are a poet," then, becomes the ultimate answer, the definition of her created and creative condition, and with this understanding, she says, "it was he himself, he who set me free / to prophesy." Her prophecy here is her passionate assertion of woman's integrity and independence and creative power, as represented in her erotic evocation of the Dancer:

> O God, what is it,
> this flower
> that in itself had power over the whole earth?
> for she needs no man,
> herself
> is that dart and pulse of the male,
> hands, feet, thighs,
> herself perfect.

One is bound to wonder who this dancer might be who has aroused so strong a response. Perhaps she is a composite figure, but one component in that figure may be the young singer-dancer-actress Anny Ahlers, whose performance in the operetta *The Dubarry* stirred H. D. to write a whole page of admiration in a letter of 1932. But the exact identification is not so significant here as it is with the other three poems in this kind, for the Dancer is observed only in performance; the symbolism arises from her role on the stage, not from any personal relationship.

What seems more certain is that H. D. in "The Poet" has paid a calm and measured tribute to the memory of D. H. Lawrence. Many of the details in this poem are private and obscure, but enough emerges to make the identification of the male poet fairly clear. "There is death / and the dead past:" she writes, "but you were not living at all / and I was half-living"— alluding apparently to the years immediately after Lawrence's death (in 1930) when her creative powers were blocked. "I don't grasp his philosophy, / and I don't understand," she says,

> but I put out a hand, touch a cold door,
> (we have both come from so far;)
> I touch something imperishable;
> I think,
> why should he stay there?
> why should he guard a shrine so alone,
> so apart,
> on a path that leads nowhere?

She is speaking in imagination before "your small coptic temple" which

is left inland,
in spite of wind,
not yet buried
in sand-storm . . .

everyone has heard of the small coptic temple,
but who knows you,
who dwell there?

Is this a reference to the "shrine" in New Mexico, the little building at the
top of a steep ascent where Frieda had placed Lawrence's ashes in April,
1935?

he couldn't live alone in the desert,
without vision to comfort him,
there must be voices somewhere.

And so she sends her voice in a final reconciliation:

I am almost afraid to speak,
certainly won't cry out, "hail,"
or "farewell" or the things people do shout:

I am almost afraid to think to myself,
why,
he is there.

It is a beautiful and significant triad, the healing Master in the center,
with the flaming tribute to the female artist on the one side, and the sad,
deeply affectionate memorial to the male artist on the other. "I had two loves
separate." Now Freud has set her free to prophesy. Her powers are restored
and prepared to face the challenge of another borderline—the London bombing of the second war, where a whole civilization stands on the edge of
destruction, where millions of ordinary people live nightly on the edge of
death—and the poet shares it all.

The uncollected poems beginning with "Body and Soul" up through
"Christmas 1944," with their careful dating in the wartime era, prepare the
way for the climax of her career, the trilogy written in 1942–44. The first
part, *The Walls Do Not Fall,* represents a series of experiments in responding
to the danger and the bravery of the scene, a sequence firmly grounded at
beginning and end in the actual experience of the bombing:

pressure on heart, lungs, the brain
about to burst its brittle case . . .

> under us, the earth sway, dip of a floor,
> slope of a pavement
>
> where men roll, drunk
> with a new bewilderment,
> sorcery, bedevilment:
>
> the bone-frame was made for
> no such shock knit within terror,
> yet the skeleton stood up to it.

But the question remains: "we passed the flame: we wonder / what saved us? what for?"

Already the opening section has begun its tacit answer to that question, as, in accord with the dedication, "for Karnack 1923 / from London 1942," the poem equates the opening of an Egyptian tomb with the "opening" of churches and other buildings by the bombs:

> there, as here, ruin opens
> the tomb, the temple; enter,
> there as here, there are no doors:
>
> the shrine lies open to the sky.

So too an opening happens in the mind, under the impact of disaster:

> ruin everywhere, yet as the fallen roof
> leaves the sealed room
> open to the air,
>
> so, through our desolation,
> thoughts stir, inspiration stalks us
> through gloom:
>
> unaware, Spirit announces the Presence.

The fourth section presents this opening in yet another way: reverting to her old Imagist technique, she picks up the image of "that craftsman, / the shell-fish," and makes it represent the tough integrity of the artist, saying, "I sense my own limit"—and yet know "the pull / of the tide."

> be firm in your own small, static, limited
>
> orbit and the shark-jaws
> of outer circumstance

> will spit you forth:
> be indigestible, hard, ungiving,
>
> so that, living within,
> you beget, self-out-of-self,
>
> selfless,
>
> that pearl-of-great-price.

This is only a beginning. From here she moves out to explore "the valley of a leaf," to remember the meaning of "Mercury, Hermes, Thoth," inventors and patrons of the Word. And then, "when the shingles hissed / in the rain of incendiary," a Voice speaks louder than the "whirr and roar in the high air," and she has her vision and dream where "Ra, Osiris, *Amen* appeared / in a spacious, bare meeting-house"—in Philadelphia or in Bethlehem, Pennsylvania:

> yet he was not out of place
> but perfectly at home
>
> in that eighteenth-century
> simplicity and grace.

As in Freud's study, all religions are blending into one in her mind, though critics, she knows, will complain that "Depth of the sub-conscious spews forth / too many incongruent monsters." Nevertheless, through word-play and all her other poetic devices, like them or not, her aim is to

> recover the secret of Isis,
> which is: there was One
>
> in the beginning, Creator,
> Fosterer, Begetter, the Same-forever
>
> in the papyrus-swamp
> in the Judean meadow.

This is all preliminary: the secret is not yet found. It is discovered in the second part, *Tribute to the Angels,* a sequence wholly unified and sustained, moving forward confidently under the guidance of Hermes Trismegistus, inventor of language, father of alchemy, founder of Egyptian culture; and with the support of the book of Revelation, in which she boldly and wittily finds her role as prophet justified:

> *I John saw. I testify;*
> *if any man shall add*
>
> *God shall add unto him the plagues,*
> *but he that sat upon the throne* said,
>
> *I make all things new.*

H. D. is remembering how the author of the book of Revelation emerges in his own voice at the very end: "For I testify unto every man that heareth the words of the prophecy of this book, If any man shall add unto these things, God shall add unto him the plagues that are written in this book"—thus denying future prophets any function. But the poet prefers to take her stand upon the words of Jesus himself, earlier in the book: "And he that sat upon the throne said, Behold, I make all things new. And he said unto me, Write: for these words are true and faithful." (21:5)

She writes because she has been privileged to witness an apocalyptic scene of war in the heavens such as no earlier generation had seen, and more than this, she has watched with all the others who

> with unbowed head, watched
> and though unaware, worshipped
>
> and knew not that they worshipped
> and that they were
>
> that which they worshipped

that is, the very spirit "of strength, endurance, anger / in their hearts." Out of all this her visions appear: "where the red-death fell / . . . the lane is empty but the levelled wall / is purple as with purple spread / upon an altar"—but this is not the sacrifice of blood: "this is the flowering of the rood, / this is the flowering of the reed." Thus in her wordplay the rod of Aaron and the cross of Christ are merged; the reed that struck Christ merges with the reed of the Nile earlier mentioned, with overtones of music and of poetry. Now the poetry shows an alchemical change, as "a word most bitter, *marah*," changes into "mer, mere, mère, mater, Maia, Mary, / Star of the Sea, / Mother," and this star changes into "Venus, Aphrodite, Astarte, / star of the east, / star of the west," as the crucible of the mind creates a jewel

> green-white, opalescent,
>
> with under-layer of changing blue,
> with rose-vein; a white agate

with a pulse uncooled that beats yet,
faint blue-violet;

it lives, it breathes,
it gives off—fragrance?

It is an image that suggests a concentration of creative power in a mind prepared to realize the miracle happening in the outer world, which now in May (Maia) is re-creating itself in the same subtle hues:

tell me, in what other place

will you find the may flowering
mulberry and rose-purple?

tell me, in what other city
will you find the may-tree

so delicate, green-white, opalescent
like our jewel in the crucible? . . .

the outer precincts and the squares
are fragrant.

Thus inner world and outer world share in this power of recreation.

In this spirit of discovery the first half of the sequence reaches a climax as she crosses a "charred portico," enters "a house through a wall," and then sees "the tree flowering; / it was an ordinary tree / in an old garden-square"—a tree "burnt and stricken to the heart," yet flowering. This was actual, "it was not a dream / yet it was vision, / it was a sign"—

a half-burnt-out apple-tree
blossoming;

this is the flowering of the rood,
this is the flowering of the wood

where, Annael, we pause to give
thanks that we rise again from death and live.

But now the dream follows, to create a higher climax, out of a dream interpreted in ways that she had learned from Freud to trust. Instead of one of the seven angels of the poem, "the Lady herself" has appeared. But who was this Lady? Was she the Virgin Mary, as painted in the Renaissance with all her grace and glory and "damask and figured brocade"? No, she was none of these, though she had something of the pagan and "gracious friendliness / of the marble sea-maids in Venice / who climb the altar-stair / at *Santa Maria dei Miracoli.*" This joyous, teasing mood is something rare in H. D., and it continues in its tantalizing way. Her "veils were *white as snow,*" to use the language of Christ's transfiguration, but in fact she bore "none of her usual attributes; / the Child was not with her." So then it was not Mary. But who then?

> she must have been pleased with us,
> for she looked so kindly at us
>
> under her drift of veils,
> and she carried a book.

This is a trap for the academic interpreter, whom she now proceeds to parody:

> Ah (you say), this is Holy Wisdom,
> *Santa Sophia,* the SS of the *Sanctus Spiritus*
>
> . . . .
>
> she brings the Book of Life, obviously.

And so on and so on. But now the poet intervenes:

> she carries a book but it is not
> the tome of the ancient wisdom,
>
> the pages, I imagine, are the blank pages
> of the unwritten volume of the new
>
> . . . .
>
> she is Psyche, the butterfly,
> out of the cocoon.

It is the spirit of the poet, reborn, reaching out toward the future, predicting its redemption, exulting in the victory of life over death.

The third part, *The Flowering of the Rod,* is more relaxed, even diffuse in places, though never out of control. Continuing her happy mood, the poet here creates a new myth of redemption by her story of how Mary Magdalen gained from Kaspar, one of the Magi, the alabaster jar from which she anointed the feet of Christ. It is a tale that reaches out now to cover all the "smouldering cities" of Europe—not only London, but other "broken" cities that need redemption, in other lands. It is a universal myth of forgiveness and healing, a parable like that of the grain of mustard-seed:

　　　the least of all seeds
　　　that grows branches

　　　where the birds rest;
　　　it is that flowering balm,

　　　it is heal-all,
　　　everlasting;

　　　it is the greatest among herbs
　　　and becometh a tree.

It is told in a manner that in places resembles a children's story—but then one remembers that it is a Christmas tale, as the date at the end reminds us: "December 18–31, 1944."

ADALAIDE MORRIS

The Concept of Projection: H. D.'s Visionary Powers

In April 1920, while staying with her friend Bryher in a hotel on the island of Corfu, H. D. had a vision which marked and measured the rest of her life. It set the aims, announced the means, and disclosed the dimensions of her great work, the visionary epics *Trilogy* and *Helen in Egypt,* and it seemed to guarantee her gift as seer and prophet. It would be twenty years from the Corfu vision to the poems that first grasp its promise, however, years of drift and anxiety in which H. D. would write and rewrite the story of her vision. By the time the event achieves final formulation in the first part of *Tribute to Freud* [hereafter referred to as *TF*], it is clear that, however charged the vision's imagery, the plot we are to follow, the *mythos* of the matter, is its method: the miraculous projection of the images.

As H. D. explains in *Tribute to Freud,* the images she witnessed had the clarity, intensity, and authenticity of dream symbols and yet took shape not inside her mind but on the wall between the foot of her bed and the washstand. Because it was late afternoon and their side of the hotel was already dim and because the images were outlined in light, the shapes that appeared could not have been cast shadows. Neither accidental nor random, they formed with a stately, steady purpose, one after another, and seemed inscribed by the same hand. Their abstract, impersonal, rather conventional notation—a head in profile, a chalice, a ladder, an angel named Victory or Niké—made them appear part of a picture-alphabet or hieroglyphic system,

From *Contemporary Literature* 25, no. 4 (Winter 1984). © 1984 by the Board of Regents of the University of Wisconsin System.

a supposition reinforced by their orderly succession, their syntax. For these reasons and because of the eerie, miraculous portentousness of the moment, H. D. calls this experience the "writing on the wall" (*TF*).

When Belshazzar witnessed the writing on his wall, he glimpsed along with the letters a part of the hand that wrote them. The origin of H. D.'s writing is, if equally mysterious, less simply formulated. The agent is not a hand but a projective process: the casting of an image onto a screen. The vision's earlier images, which appear entire, are like magic lantern slides; the later ones, which draw themselves in dots of light elongating into lines, resemble primitive movies.

The path from mind to wall is direct. It at first seems to follow what H. D. calls her "sustained crystal-gazing stare" (*TF*), an aching concentration that propels the image outward on her eyebeam. Because the vision rides on will, she must not flag: "if I let go," she thinks, "lessen the intensity of my stare and shut my eyes or even blink my eyes, to rest them, the pictures will fade out" (*TF*). When, however, she drops her head in her hands, exhausted, the process continues and Bryher, who has until now seen nothing, witnesses the final image. What she sees—H. D.'s Niké elevated into the sun-disk—is so consistent with the preceding figures that H. D. compares it to "that 'determinative' that is used in the actual hieroglyph, the picture that contains the whole series of pictures in itself or helps clarify or explain them" (*TF*). With the power of the poet or prophet, H. D. has not only materialized the images of her psyche but cast them onto the consciousness of another and released her audience's own visionary capacities.

The images of the vision are described as flowing from, or at least through, H. D.'s psyche, yet their origin is obscured. What creates these slides or magic transparencies? Where do they come from? The answer given in *Tribute to Freud* is ambiguous. On the one hand, the images seem little different than the clips from memories or dream-scenes that H. D. had earlier compared to "transparencies in a dark room, set before lighted candles" (*TF*). In this sense, however extraordinary, they would be "merely an extension of the artist's mind, a *picture* or an illustrated poem, taken out of the actual dream or daydream content and projected from within" (*TF*). On the other hand, in an interpretation H. D. clearly prefers, one sanctioned by the classical belief that gods speak through dreams and oracles, the images seem "projected from outside" (*TF*), messages from another world, another state of being.

Images as signs and warnings from her own subconscious, images as signs and wonders from another world; the artist as moving-picture machine, the artist as psychic, the artist as message-transmitter: what gives this odd combination of attributes unity and coherence, positions it within H. D.'s development, and makes it central to any interpretation of her work is the concept of projection. All the more apt for its abundant ambiguities, projection is the master metaphor of H. D.'s technique. Its operations connect the material, mental, and mystical realms and enact her belief that there is no physical reality that is not also psychic and spiritual. Without the energies of projection, H. D.'s work stalls and thins; with them, her writing has strength and brilliance. It is this excellence that the "projected pictures" at Corfu seem to promise.

The word *projection* appears throughout H. D.'s work. Though its meaning alters subtly and sometimes confusingly, it always marks an important moment in her creative process. From the verb meaning *to throw forward*, projection is the thrust that bridges two worlds. It is the movement across a borderline: between the mind and the wall, between the brain and the page, between inner and outer, between me and you, between states of being, across dimensions of time and space. The concept of projection informs H. D.'s transitions from Imagist to clairvoyant, to film theorist, analysand, and prophetic poet. What does it clarify at each stage? how does it change between stages? what light does it throw on the overall strategies and strengths of H. D.'s work? These will be the questions that guide our inquiry.

Projection: the act of throwing or shooting forward

"Cut the cackle!" "Go in fear of abstractions!" "Don't be 'viewy'!" Most memorable Imagist statements are prescriptions against a poetic tradition condemned as rigid, overblown, and unoriginal. Cackle is the chatter of conventional verse. It fills long lines with flourishes [Ezra] Pound called "rhetorical bustuous rumpus": platitudes, circumlocutions, and rolling, ornamental din. To theorists like Pound and T. E. Hulme, these flourishes were self-generated and self-sustained, cut off from the world they purported to present. In its eagerness to pronounce upon the world and in the vaporous grandeur of its pronouncements, cackle went in fear neither of abstractions nor of viewiness.

The cure for cackle is contact. Imagist theory privileges sight as fresh, accurate access to the exterior world. Sight is the acid bath that dissolves the sticky sludge of rhetoric. It connects us directly, so the Imagists argue, with the things of this world. Bad art, for Hulme, is "words divorced from any real vision," strings of conventional locutions, abstractions, "counters" which, like "x" and "y" in an algebraic formula, replace six pounds of cashews and four Florida oranges. Formulaic words, like algebraic symbols, can be manipulated according to laws independent of their meaning. Hulme's test of good poetry is whether the words turn back into things that we can see.

The major Imagist theorists echo each other on this point. "Each *word* must be an image *seen,* not a counter," Hulme legislates. "Language in a healthy state," T. S. Eliot insists, "presents the object, is so close to the object that the two are identical." For Pound, "the very essence" of a writer's work is "the application of word to thing." It was Pound who discovered, through the work of Ernest Fenollosa, the ur-pattern of the word-thing: the Chinese ideogram which was assumed to be direct, visibly concrete, natural rather than conventional, a picture language within which, as Fenollosa put it, "Thinking is *thinging.*"

The image of a thing, set into a poem, becomes for the Imagists the innocent word, the word that has somehow escaped the conventional, abstracting, mediating nature of language. The assumption of transparent expression is a correlate of the Bergsonian faith in the artist's direct intuition of the object. Where contemporary theorists hold that we see what we know, Imagists insist we know what we see. They find in vision the release from a shared system of signs into spontaneous, intuitive, unmediated apprehension of essences. Whatever her subsequent elaborations—and they are many and strange—this belief in the possibility of essential intuitions, so central to Imagism, remains at the core of H. D.'s projective practice.

Projection is the act of throwing or shooting forward. Though the Imagists don't use the term, they depend on the concept. In the genesis of the Imagist poem, a thing in the world projects its essence onto the poet's consciousness; the poet imprints the image, or record of the thing, in a poem; and the poem, in turn, projects the image onto the reader's consciousness. The model for this, the simplest form of projection, is the magic lantern show. It is Hulme's concrete display of images that "always endeavours to arrest you, and to make you continuously see a physical thing"; it is Pound's *phanopoeia,* the technique by which "you use a word to throw a visual concept on to the reader's imagination."

H. D.'s *Sea Garden* is full of *phanopoeia.* The reader's visual imagination is bombarded by sand, tree-bark, salt tracks, silver dust, wood violets, and thin, stinging twigs—objects in a world of clear, hard-edged, gritty particularity. The images have an almost hallucinatory specificity. The view is tight, close-up, almost too bright: on the beach, "hard sand breaks, / and the grains of it / are clear as wine"; in the late afternoon sun, "each leaf / cuts another leaf on the grass"; night, when it comes, curls "the petals / back from the stalk / . . . under till the rinds break, / back till each bent leaf / is parted from its stalk." Break, cut, curl: these moments are doubly projective. H. D.'s images, forcibly cast onto the reader's imagination, themselves record moments in which one thing, thrown onto another, opens, releases, or transforms it. In *Sea Garden*, objects are perpetually twisted, lifted, flung, split, scattered, slashed, and stripped clear by rushing energies that enact the impact the poet wishes to exert on the reader's imagination.

The rushing energies are the sea, the sun, and the night, but in H. D.'s world these are more than fierce weather: they testify to a sacred power and promise in the universe. Unlike other of the Imagists, H. D. conceived of essence as god-stuff. To her, each intense natural fact is the trace of a spiritual force; each charged landscape enshrines a deity. Thus, in *Sea Garden*, dryads haunt the groves, nereids the waves; Priapus transfuses the orchard, Artemis courses the woods; Hermes marks the crossroads, and the mysterious Wind Sleepers roam searching for their altar. The world glows with sacred energy.

This radiance, however, like a Derridean sign, marks a presence that is vanished or just vanishing. Gods do not manifest directly to mortals, but they do, like Apollo at Delphi, leave us signs, the afterglow of sacred presence. The speaker in *Sea Garden* is a supplicant in search of deities that are everywhere immanent in the landscape: they beckon, stand tense, await us a moment, then surge away, leaving behind heel prints, snapped stalks, and a charged silence. The poet, like a skilled tracker, moves from sign to sign in rapt, sagacious pursuit.

As embodiments of essence, the deities might seem mere metaphors, relics of the kind of claptrap the Imagists despised. H. D.'s work, however, is spare, stripped, as Pound said, of slither. In it, the gods function not as the poems' ornament but as their absent center. The deities are both cause and condition of this poetry; the poems do not work if we don't posit the reality of the presence they yearn toward.

The poems in *Sea Garden* are thrown out as bridges to the sacred. They project themselves toward the gods with a plea that the gods will in return appear to us. Poems like "Sea Gods," "Hermes of the Ways," "The Helmsman," and "The Shrine" address the gods directly, compelling them from immanence to manifestation: "For you will come," H. D. presses, "you will come, / you will answer our taut hearts, / . . . and cherish and shelter us." Projection as *phanopoeia*, a poetic technique, here, in H. D.'s first important modification, broadens into a technique of meditation or prayer: an imaging used to summon a being from another world.

Projection: a representation on a plane surface
of any part of the celestial sphere

Except for three brief reviews in *The Egoist,* H. D. took little part in the barrage of Imagist treatises and evaluations. Contrasting strongly with the polemics she later wrote for the cinema, this silence had several sources. She was a new poet, unused to literary disputation, and, until the arrival of Amy Lowell, she was the only woman in a contentious group of men. In addition, she held a constricted position in the movement: if Hulme was its principal theorist and Pound its chief publicist, H. D. was from the first the Imagiste extraordinaire, the movement's most effective practitioner. Her poems stimulated and exemplified positions held by others.

A third, more significant source of H. D.'s silence, however, lies in her hesitations about Imagist doctrine. Her *Egoist* review of John Gould Fletcher's *Goblins and Pagodas,* for example, makes an obligatory bow to Imagist principles but is compelled by something else. "He uses the direct image, it is true," H. D. writes, "but he seems to use it as a means of evoking other and vaguer images—a pebble, as it were, dropped into a quiet pool, in order to start across the silent water, wave on wave of light, of colour, of sound." Fletcher attempts "a more difficult and, when successfully handled, richer form of art: not that of direct presentation, but that of suggestion." The goblins and pagodas that title his volume testify to visionary capacities. His art pursues not the solidity of physical things so much as the spiritual enigmas that radiate from them.

The next stage of H. D.'s development furthers her own shift from pebbles to their radiating rings: from the objects of this world to the phantasms of light, color, and sound surrounding them; from our three dimensions to the largest ring of all, the fourth dimension or celestial sphere surrounding us. In 1919, after her bonds with Pound, Aldington, and the other Imagists had cracked, after her alliance with Bryher had begun and her daughter Perdita had been born, H. D. had a series of intense psychic experiences. The visions of 1919 and 1920 undid any remaining traces of Imagist empiricism, affirmed a privileged role for the woman poet, and demonstrated H. D.'s clairvoyant powers. Applied to these experiences, the term *projection* registers not the poet's design on the reader or on the gods but rather the dynamics of clairvoyance. To this end H. D. extends the term by borrowing a metaphor from the art of cartography.

In the language of mapping, projection is the representation of a sphere on a flat surface. Like most figuration, projection simplifies, here reducing a curve to a plane. Two methods of charting the heavens clarify the distinction between general and cartographic projection. In the first sense, as Robert Duncan in *The H. D. Book* observes, we make the night "a projected screen" by casting our mythologies into the heavens and rendering "the sky-dome above . . . the image of another configuration in the skull-dome below."

Cartographers reverse this movement and project intersecting coordinate lines from the sky down to our earthly charts. This entry of another dimension into our familiar figuration is the equivalent in H. D.'s work of the process by which material from the celestial or astral planes manifests on the earthly plane. It is this that haunts and compels her.

H. D. experienced what she felt was an inrush of material from other dimensions at least four times in 1919–1920, all after surviving her near-fatal childbirth and all in the steadying company of Bryher. The first, in late spring 1919, involved "the transcendental feeling of the two globes or the two transparent half-globes enclosing me" (*TF*); the second was the apparition of an ideal figure on the voyage to Greece in 1920; the third and fourth, in the hotel room at Corfu, were the projected pictures and a series of dance scenes conjured up for Bryher. Each of these seemed, as H. D. affirmed, "a god-send," an irradiation of the world of ordinary events and rules by an extraordinary grace.

The first of these experiences is described in *Notes on Thought and Vision* [hereafter referred to as *NTV*], a document composed for Havelock Ellis, whom H. D. and Bryher had been consulting and who subsequently accompanied them to Greece. Though rough and sometimes contradictory, these notes describe a matrix of creativity she calls the "jelly-fish" or "over-mind" state (*NTV*). The self is divided into body, mind, and over-mind. The artist-initiate begins, like the neophyte in the Eleusinian mysteries, with the body's desires and the brain's sensitivities, but the aim is to transcend these consciousnesses in the over-mind, the receptacle of mystical vision.

Like Ellis, H. D. begins her exposition with sexuality. All humans need physical relationships, she argues, but creative men and women crave them "to develop and draw forth their talents" (*NTV*). The erotic personality, suffused with sympathetic, questing, and playful energies, is the artistic personality par excellence, a hypothesis Ellis and H. D. both exemplify by evoking Leonardo da Vinci. Ellis, however, separates sexuality's primary reproductive function from a secondary spiritual function of "furthering the higher mental and emotional processes." H. D. counters this separation with a theory derived partly from the Eleusinian mysteries and partly from her own recent childbirth.

Complementing the "vision of the brain" is a force H. D. calls "vision of the womb" (*NTV*). The term underscores the artist's receptive/procreative role. In the womb-brain, thoughts from another realm are received, nourished, brought to form, then projected out into the barrenness H. D. calls "the murky, dead, old, thousand-times explored old world" (*NTV*). This model rewrites conventional phallic metaphors for creativity by depicting visionary consciousness as "a foetus in the body" which, after "grinding discomfort," is released in the miracle the mysteries celebrated as Kore's return. "Is it easier for a woman to attain this state of consciousness than for a man?" H. D. asks. Though both sexes possess this capacity, her formulation privileges her own particularly female experience of integration and regeneration (NTV).

Notes on Thought and Vision provides many explications of visionary consciousness, but the most pertinent to H. D.'s developing notion of projection are three ocular models. H. D.'s fascination with optics came from watching her father the astronomer and her grandfather the botanist gaze through lenses into a teeming world where before there had been only a blank. Each of her models postulates two kinds of vision, womb vision and brain vision, and each invents a way to adjust them so as to transform void to plenitude.

H. D.'s initial formulation describes the jellyfish state as enclosure in two caps or diving bells of consciousness, one over the forehead and one in the "love region." Each is a sort of amniotic sac, "like water, transparent, fluid yet with definite body, contained in a definite space . . . like a closed sea-plant, jelly-fish or anemone." This sac holds and nurtures the delicate, amorphous life of the over-mind, but it has a further function. Like a diver's mask or aquarium glass, the over-mind allows us to see the usually invisible inhabitants of the watery depths: here, H. D. explains, "thoughts pass and are visible like fish swimming under clear water" (NTV).

The second formulation transforms these caps into dual lenses for a pair of psychic opera glasses. These, "properly adjusted, focused . . . bring the world of vision into consciousness. The two work separately, perceive separately, yet make one picture" (NTV). What they see is the whole world of vision registered by the mystic, the philosopher, and the artist.

In the last and most evocative formulation, these lenses merge into a complexly constituted third eye. "The jelly-fish over my head," H. D. explains, "had become concentrated. . . . That is, all the spiritual energy seemed concentrated in the middle of my forehead, inside my skull, and it was small and giving out a very soft light, but not scattered light, light concentrated in itself as the light of a pearl would be" (NTV). Like a crystal ball, this eye both receives and emits the force H. D. calls "over-world energy" (NTV). It draws in, concentrates, then projects outward "pictures from the world of vision" (NTV). This receptive/transmissive eye is the gift of vision, the pearl of great price.

The jellyfish eye opens the skull-dome. Into, out of, through this rupture pours all the prophetic soul-energy scientific materialism would deny and

H. D.'s visions and visionary poetry affirm. Archetypal memories, dreams, the Corfu pictures all exemplify this projected vision, but a more excessive, startling instance is the sudden apparition of Peter Van Eck at the shiprail of the Borodino.

For more than twenty years, H. D. struggled to tell the story of Peter Van Eck, her code name for Peter Rodeck, architect, artist, spiritualist, and fellow passenger on the voyage to Greece. It formed the heart of a much rewritten novel entitled Niké, finally jettisoned in 1924. The most ample remaining accounts are in the pseudonymous short story "Mouse Island," published in 1932; in the analysis notebooks of 1933, published as part of Tribute to Freud; and in the unpublished autobiographical novel The Majic Ring, written in 1943–44.

It was sunset, neither day nor night, and the ocean was suffused with a soft violet-blue glow. The ship was approaching the Pillars of Hercules between the outer-waters of the Atlantic and the inner-sea of the Mediter-ranean. "We were crossing something," H. D. explains—a line, a boundary, perhaps a threshold (TF). Alone at the rail of the Borodino, she stood "on the deck of a mythical ship as well, a ship that had no existence in the world of ordinary events and laws and rules." The sea was quiet, the boat moved smoothly, and the waves broke "in a thousand perfectly peaked wavelets like the waves in the background of a Botticelli" (TF). When she turned to search for Bryher, she saw a three-dimensional figure at the rail, a man who both was and was not Peter Van Eck. Taller, clearer, brighter than Van Eck, with-out his disfiguring scar and thick-rimmed glasses, this apparition summoned a band of leaping dolphins and disclosed, on the ship's seaward side, a chain of hilly islands. At the peak of the moment, H. D. reports, "his eyes, it seemed now, were my eyes. I was seeing his vision, what he (though I did not of course, realize it) was himself projecting. This was the promised land, the islands of the blest, the islands of Atlantis or of the Hesperides."

Was this a hallucination, a holographic illusion, an epiphany? If the latter, who was the being who directed or even impersonated Peter Van Eck? H. D. gives no consistent answer. The Majic Ring suggests it was "Anax Apollo, Helios, Lord of Magic and Prophecy and Music"; the letters to Silvia Dobson imply he was an astral double; the story "Mouse Island" compares him to Christ at Emmaus.

Whatever he was, all accounts agree he was a "projection" from another dimension into this one, a phenomenon for which "Mouse Island" gives the most extensive—and mechanical—explication. If each being is composed of two substances, "platinum sheet-metal over jellyfish" or body over soul, Van Eck's appearance was a "galvanized projection": soul-stuff shocked into form, transmitted through the third-eye opening in his skull, perceived through the opening in hers. "The inside could get out that way," the story tells us, "only when the top was broken. It was the transcendentalist inside that had met [Van Eck] in the storm on deck, when [Peter Van Eck] was downstairs in the smoking room."

The terminology is awkward, the physics creak, but the experience was real and haunted H. D. all her life. Van Eck's three-dimensionality was a kind of psychic *phanopoeia*—not at all what Pound meant but very much H. D.'s technique in her later poetry. The visionary figures of *Trilogy*, the hordes of souls thronging *Helen in Egypt,* the angelic forces of *Hermetic Definition,* all are figures entering the imagination from another dimension and carrying with them the mysterious radiance by which H. D. gratefully remapped our "dead, old, thousand-times explored old world."

Projection: the display of motion pictures by
casting an image on a screen

When H. D. once again broached the Greek material in the 1940s, she reported that "the story, in its new form, began unwinding itself, like a roll of film that had been neatly stored in my brain, waiting for a propitious moment to be re-set in the projector and cast on a screen." This new twist to the term *projection* emerged from extensive experience. She had taken an exhilarating step into the technology of the cinema.

In spring 1929, when asked by *The Little Review* what she most liked to do, H. D. had no trouble answering. "I myself have learned to use the small projector," she replied, "and spend literally hundreds of hours alone in my apartment, making the mountains and village streets and my own acquaintances reel past me in the light and light and light." The projector belonged to POOL Productions, a company run by Bryher and Kenneth Macpherson, H. D.'s companions in film work in the late 1920s and early 1930s. H. D. wrote for their journal *Close Up,* acted in their films, did montage for one and publicity for two, and, finally, filled her contemporary poetry and fiction with images of light, focus, superimposition, and projection.

Most of H. D.'s film theory is in a series of essays composed for the first issues of *Close Up* and titled "The Cinema and the Classics." By "classics" H. D. meant, specifically, Greek culture and, more narrowly, the Greek amalgamation of the beautiful and the good. Despite Hollywood's fixation on "longdrawn out embraces and the artificially enhanced thud-offs of galloping bronchoes" and despite "the gigantic Cyclops, the American Censor" who prettifies beauty and homogenizes goodness, cinema offers our best opportunity to recapture Greek wisdom. In the hands of the avant-garde, film repossesses the visionary consciousness of Athens, Delphi, and Eleusis. Here, at last, "miracles and godhead are *not* out of place, are not awkward"; it is "a perfect medium . . . at last granted us."

The word *medium* resonates through H. D.'s meditations. Film is an artistic medium, one occupying a medial position between the filmmaker's visual imagination and our own, but for H. D. it also functions as a psychic medium externalizing and making perceptible invisible inward intentions and coherencies. The announcement of the POOL film *Wing Beat*, starring H. D. and Kenneth Macpherson, promises "Telepathy and attraction, the reaching out, the very edge of dimensions in dimensions." Film reads and reveals the far reaches of our minds, and this connects it for H. D. with the Delphian dictate "Know Thyself." The mediumship, however, is more than telepathic. Cinema discloses the thoughts of the gods, their power, knowledge, and beauty. It may even, finally, disclose their very being, for here "Hermes, indicated in faint light, may step forward, outlined in semi-obscurity, or simply dazzling the whole picture in a blaze of splendour. Helios may stand simply and restrained with uplifted arm."

Because film calls together in a dark room witnesses of charged hieratic images, images that make manifest what was mysterious, because it brings light to darkness and conveys the will of beauty and goodness, cinema is to us what the church was to H. D.'s ancestors and what the Delphic oracle was to the Greeks. The long two-part poem H. D. entitled "Projector" and published alongside her essays in *Close Up* names the Delphian Apollo as god of the cinema and envisions him reasserting his domain on a ray of image-bearing, world-creating light:

> This is his gift;
> light,
> light
> a wave
> that sweeps
> us
> from old fears
> and powers.

Just as Apollo claimed the power of prophecy at Delphi by slaying the monster Python, this projector-god destroys squalid commercialism and makes Hollywood into a "holy wood" where "souls upon the screen / live lives that might have been, / live lives that ever are."

H. D.'s ecstatic poem greets Apollo as he begins his miracles. The poem's clipped, incantatory lines and detailed invocation of the Delphic paradigm, however, suggest something more than simple salutation. H. D.'s advocacy asserts a place and function for herself. Apollo at Delphi works through his oracle, the Pythoness, who is a medium between the god and the seeker. She has what *Notes on Thought and Vision* calls "womb vision," for it is she who receives, brings to form, and throws forth his knowledge. As the transmitter of the prophetic message, her position precedes and predicts H. D.'s. Who, then, is the poem's "Projector"? It is Apollo, light-bearer; it is his Delphic oracle; it is H. D. herself, the projector-poet; and perhaps it is also the machine in her apartment which, in a coincidence that doubtless delighted H. D., rested, like the Pythoness herself, upon a tripod— symbol of prophecy, prophetic utterance, occult or hidden knowledge.

> *Projection: a defense mechanism in which the*
> *individual attributes an impulse of*
> *his own to some other person or object*
> *in the outside world*

 Close Up did not push a particular doctrine. It contained accounts of German and Russian cinema, translations of Eisenstein, reviews of film exhibitions and avant-garde screenings, vituperations against Hollywood's censor, advice on the newest cameras and projectors, and assorted editorial pronouncements. As Anne Friedberg notes, however, one consistent strain in its pages is psychoanalytic theory. Many of the writers cite Freud; Dr. Hanns Sachs, Bryher's analyst and a member of Freud's inner circle, and lay analysts Barbara Low and Mary Chadwick contribute essays; and editor Kenneth Macpherson frequently elaborates his positions with psychoanalytic concepts. This interest illuminates Macpherson's own most ambitious project, the full-length film *Borderline,* in which H. D., disguised in the credits as Helga Doorn, plays a character caught between conscious and unconscious pressures. Her work on *Borderline* provides a glimpse into H. D.'s preoccupations some three years prior to her analysis with Freud.

 Macpherson intended to take the film "into the labyrinth of the human mind, with its queer impulses and tricks, its unreliability, its stresses and obsessions, its half-formed deductions, its glibness, its occasional amnesia, its fantasy, suppression, and desires." The plot is a tangle of desire, murder, and bigotry. Astrid, the sensitive and worldly neurotic played by H. D., comes with her alcoholic husband Thorne to a small Swiss border town; in this limbo, she becomes obsessed with Pete, a giant, half-vagrant black man played by Paul Robeson, and is stabbed to death by Thorne in a crime for which the town persecutes Pete. The frayed atmosphere is exacerbated by the movie's silence, by the camera's raking of symbolic landscapes and faces gouged with light, and, finally, by Astrid's staring into the camera—as if she were emptying her mind out onto the screen, or, even more uncomfortably, as if she were attempting a direct transfer of her psychic content into the mind of the viewer.

The unsigned, thirty-nine page publicity pamphlet, almost certainly written by H. D., reminds us that "Astrid, the woman, terribly incarnated, is 'astral' in effect." The earthly/astral border is only one more in a film deliberately situated on every possible margin: physical, social, racial, sexual, mental, even, since Macpherson and his company were displaced and uncredentialed, professional. The film's terrain is the limbo that H. D.'s projection—Imagist, clairvoyant, cinematic, or prophetic—always traversed.

If the stark, otherworldly sequences that punctuate *Borderline* have a hieroglyphic portentousness, it is because they in fact originated in picture-writing. As the pamphlet explains, Macpherson drew 910 pen-and-ink sketches giving detailed directions for each shot. Each was a light sculpture, a dream scene, a hieroglyph designed for projection, a "welding of the psychic or super-normal to the things of precise everyday existence." For H. D. this places *Borderline* in the same psychic category as the Corfu pictures and the charged dreams of her accounts of analysis: "For myself," she writes in *Tribute to Freud,* "I consider this sort of dream or projected picture or vision as a sort of halfway state between ordinary dream and the vision of those who, for lack of a more definite term, we must call psychics or clairvoyants" (*TF*).

"Borderline" is, of course, a psychoanalytic term designating the halfway state between neurosis and psychosis. H. D. would know the term from Bryher, who in the 1920s was both studying and undergoing analysis, from lectures she and Bryher attended in Berlin during these years, from the general theoretic climate of *Close Up,* and, finally, from the fact that Macpherson in titling his film doubtless had the technical term in mind. While playing on all its other nuances, however, the pamphlet shuns the psychoanalytic meaning and resituates the borderline so that it lies not between the neurotic and the psychotic but between the neurotic and the psychic. This gesture typifies H. D.'s complex attitude toward psychoanalysis.

"*Borderline* is a dream," the pamphlet pronounces, entering its summation, "and perhaps when we say that we have said everything. The film is the art of dream portrayal and perhaps when we say that we have achieved the definition, the synthesis toward which we have been striving." For H. D., dream was always interior projection, a cinematic exhibition of the mind's submerged content. Like *Borderline* and the Corfu pictures, dreams display "the *hieroglyph of the unconscious*." It is for "open[ing] the field to the study of this vast, unexplored region" that H. D. would be forever grateful to Freud.

Accounts of dreams are, as it were, projections of projections, and H. D. was justly proud of her command of this intricate transmutation. It was not simple. "The dream-picture focussed and projected by the mind, may perhaps achieve something of the character of a magic-lantern slide and may 'come true' in the projection," H. D. explains in *The Gift,* but to make it do so demands all the equipment developed by Freud: free association, command of the parallels between individual, biological, and racial development, and mastery of concepts like condensation, displacement, dramatization by visual imagery, superimposition, distortion, and screen memory. An admonitory passage from *The Gift* conveys H. D.'s delight in her descriptive skill:

> The dream, the memory, the unexpected related memories must be allowed to sway backward and forward, as if the sheet or screen upon which they are projected, blows and is rippled in the wind of whatever emotion or idea is entering a door, left open. The wind blows through the door, from outside, through long, long corridors of personal memory, of biological and of race-memory. Shut the door and you have a neat flat picture. Leave all the doors open and you are almost out-of-doors, almost within the un-walled province of the fourth-dimensional. This is creation in the truer sense, in *the wind bloweth where it listeth* way.

Her delight was matched—perhaps even sparked—by Freud's joy in the intense and haunting dreams of her two periods of analysis in 1933 and 1934. "[Freud] has embarrassed me," H. D. writes Bryher in April 1933, "by telling me I have a rare type of mind he seldom meets with, in which thought crystalizes out in dream in a very special way." In their sessions they pore over dream after enigmatic dream, Freud complimenting her on their "very 'beautiful' construction," their invention of symbols, their "almost perfect mythological state." The fact that so much of H. D.'s post-analysis writing places her before a luminous dream that she both creates and analyzes, participates in and watches, surely repeats the exhilaration of her contact with Freud.

In the analysis of her dreams, H. D. and Freud are colleagues who heed, adjust, and validate each other's interpretations, but much of the analysis material indicates another kind of relationship. Here H. D. is a small, confused seeker and Freud is the wise Hermit on the edge of the Forest of the Unknown (*TF*), Asklepios the blameless healer (*TF*), Herakles struggling with Death (*TF*), Jeremiah discovering the well of living water (*TF*), St. Michael who will slay the Dragon of her fears (*TF*), even the infinitely old symbol weighing Psyche the soul in the Balance (*TF*), even the Supreme Being (*TF*). These formulations, as Freud taught us, call on another sort of projection: transference, or the process by which the patient directs toward the physician an intensity of feeling that is based on no real relation between them and can only be traced back to old fantasies rendered unconscious.

The first step in analysis, the establishment of transference, H. D. took easily, if somewhat ambiguously. To H. D., Freud became papa, the Professor, his study, like Professor Doolittle's, cluttered with erudite writings and "sacred objects" (*TF*); to Freud, however, transference made him the gentle, intuitive mother. Both were right, for as Susan Friedman points out, "in an ultimate sense, he became both mother and father to her as he fused her mother's art and her father's science in the mysteries of psychoanalysis." Her transference love for Freud enabled H. D. to affirm herself as poet and visionary, release her blocked creativity, and write with passion and continuity throughout the rest of her life.

There was another, murkier transference in the analysis, however, one subject not to resolution but to repetition. This rendered every figure in her life a stand-in for someone else, every love a deflection, every trauma a replay of earlier disaster. The records of analysis swarm with formulae as Freud and H. D. decipher originary patterns beneath a palimpsest of repetition. Ellis as father, Freud as mother; Aldington as father, Bryher as mother; Rodeck as father, Bryher as mother; her "ideal" brothers Rodeck, Frances Gregg, and Bryher; her "real" brothers Pound, Aldington, and Macpherson—the list goes on and on. One fevered letter to Bryher in March 1933 indicates both the exuberance and the suspicion of futility beneath all this activity:

> My triangle is mother-brother-self. That is, early phallic-mother, baby brother or smaller brother and self. I have worked in and around that, I have HAD the baby with my mother, and been the phallic-baby, hence Moses in the bulrushes, I have HAD the baby with the brother, hence Cuthbert [Aldington], Cecil Grey, Kenneth etc. I have HAD the "illumination" or the back to the womb WITH the brother, hence you and me in Corfu, island = mother. . . . Well, well, well, I could go on and on, demonstrating but once you get the first idea, all the other, later diverse-looking

> manifestations fit in somehow. Savvy?????? It's all too queer and
> at first, I felt life had been wasted in all this repetition etc. but
> somehow F. seems to find it amusing, sometimes.

Until the end of her life, H. D. deluged near strangers with intensities of feeling belonging not to them but to their forerunners or even to the forerunners of their forerunners. Here transference was a condition not of cure but of compulsion.

Dreams and transference are projective in a general sense, but psychoanalytic theory, of course, defines the term *projection* precisely: as a defense mechanism that causes us to attribute an interior wish to a person or object in the exterior world. This charged term formed an exemplary site for the disagreement between Freud and H. D. about the nature of reality, and here H. D. took Freud on, if not directly, nonetheless deftly.

The word *projection* occurs frequently in *Tribute to Freud,* but, like "borderline" in the movie pamphlet, not once with its Freudian denotation. The "projected picture" (*TF*), images "projected" from the subconscious mind or from outside (*TF*), the strain of projection (*TF*), the impact that "projected" a dream-sequence (*TF*): each use of the term points to the Corfu vision. Of all the events that could have titled H. D.'s original account of analysis, her choice, "Writing on the Wall," privileges and gives biblical sanction to the vision at Corfu. The phrase draws our attention from the analytic to the mystical and prepares our confrontation with the main question raised by the Corfu pictures. Were they, as Freud maintained, a "dangerous 'symptom'" (*TF*), or were they rather an upwelling of creativity, an inspiration, and a promise?

In Freud's use of the word, the "projected pictures" reduce to defensive exteriorizations of unconscious material. In this sense they would be desperate strategies of containment. By H. D.'s definition, however, the projected pictures are precisely the opposite: they open the boundaries of the self to another, higher reality, not in order to deny its operations but in order to claim and be claimed by them. The pictures predict—or project into the future—not a repetition of palimpsestic transferences but a transcendence, a breakthrough into a new dimension. In her final image, the angel Niké moving through a field of tents, H. D. recognizes the aftermath of the next world war: "When that war had completed itself," she writes, "rung by rung or year by year, I, personally (I felt), would be free, I myself would go on in another, a winged dimension" (*TF*). This vision of 1920, recalled and reaffirmed through analysis with Freud, predicts the transmutations wrought two decades later in the great poem H. D. would call her *War Trilogy.*

Projection: the casting of some ingredient into
a crucible; especially in alchemy, the
casting of the powder of the philosopher's
stone (powder of projection) *upon a metal*
in fusion to effect its transmutation
into gold or silver

H. D.'s "Notes on Recent Writing," composed in 1949 for Norman Holmes Pearson, stress the generation of *Trilogy* out of the ravages of World War Two. Throughout the Nazi air assault, H. D. had remained in London, close to the Hyde Park anti-aircraft batteries and in the thick of incendiary raids. Bombs—buzz bombs, fly bombs, oil bombs, doodle-bugs, and low, close V-1 rockets—in often nightly bombardments tore open apartments, leveled buildings, lodged unexploded shells in areaways and under pavements, and threw the survivors into unregistered dimensions of terror and power-lessness. "The fire has raged around the crystal," H. D. reported to Pearson. "The crystalline poetry to be projected, must of necessity, have that fire in it. You will find fire in *The Walls Do Not Fall, Tribute to the Angels* and *The Flowering of the Rod. Trilogy,* as we called the three volumes of poetry written during War II, seemed to project itself in time and out-of-time to-gether. And with no effort."

After agonized blockage, H. D. was writing with assurance and speed, her typewriter clacking across the noise of the raids. In the last eight months of 1944 alone she composed three of her finest works: from May 17 to 31, *Tribute to the Angels;* from September 19 to November 2, "Writing on the Wall"; from December 18 to 31, *The Flowering of the Rod.* The Freud memoir slid easily between the last two parts of *Trilogy,* for *Trilogy* performs, in its way, a kind of analysis. If, as Robert Duncan suggests (in *The H. D. Book*), "in Freudian terms, the War is a manifestation of the latent content of the civilization and its discontents, a projection of the collective uncon-scious," *Trilogy* works to surface the terrors and redirect savage impulses to sublimer ends.

As in analysis, dream is the agent of transmutation. *Trilogy,* however, builds on a distinction made in "Writing on the Wall" between "trivial, confused dreams and . . . real dreams. The trivial dream bears the same relationship to the real as a column of gutter-press newsprint to a folio page of a play of Shakespeare." The enigmas of revelatory dreams emerge not from extravagantly repressed desire but from "the same source as the script or Scripture, the Holy Writ or Word" (*TF*). Dream is the active force of the

sacred in human life. "Now it appears very clear," H. D. writes, "that the
Holy Ghost, / childhood's mysterious enigma, / is the Dream":

> it merges the distant future
> with most distant antiquity,
>
> states economically
> in a simple dream-equation
>
> the most profound philosophy,
> discloses the alchemist's secret
>
> and follows the Mage
> in the desert.

Each of the three parts of *Trilogy* generates a real dream, a vision of eternal
beings who reappear with the recovery of "the alchemist's secret," the process through which destruction precedes and permits new, more perfect life.

War executes a horrifying reverse alchemy. Rails are melted down and
made into guns, books are pulped for cartridge cases, the Word is absorbed
in the Sword, and people become "wolves, jackals, / mongrel curs" (*Trilogy*).
Casting back to "most distant antiquity" in order to project "the distant
future," H. D. turns to the early alchemists. Though our culture cartoons
them as greedy bunglers struggling to turn dung into gold, alchemists were
scholars of spiritual transformation. Alchemical formulas and philosophy
structure *Trilogy* and give the metaphor of *projection* its final precise and
complex elaboration.

Until modern chemistry's mechanical and quantitative postulates replaced alchemy's organic, qualitative theory, four tenets seemed self-evident.
The universe, alchemists believed, was everywhere alive, all matter possessing
body, passion, and soul. Because substances appear, grow, decay, diminish,
and disappear, secondly, transmutation is considered the essence of life.
Third, all transmutation moves toward perfection: the seed becomes a tree,
the worm turns into a butterfly, grains of sand round into pearls. In this
process, the seed splits, the worm bursts, the sand vanishes, thus demon-
strating the fourth alchemical tenet: the belief that all creation requires an
initial act of destruction.

Projection is the final stage of an alchemical transmutation, the act that
precipitates new, more perfect form. All *Trilogy* moves toward the moment
of projection, but to understand this moment we must look briefly at the
alchemists' explication of transformation. Like Aristotle, they believed that

each substance consists of indeterminate prime matter and specific form impressed into it like a hot seal in wax. Changing a substance, therefore, was simply a matter of altering its "form." Ingredients were cast into a crucible, heated, and, in a process alchemists called "death" or "putrefaction," reduced to prime matter; then, after many intricate maneuvers—calcination, distillation, sublimation, fermentation, separation, and more—the specific form of a finer substance was projected into the crucible and new shape sprang forth. However audacious or even preposterous this procedure might now appear, to the alchemists it merely hastened a natural, universal process.

The magical act—or, as H. D. would remind us, the act of the Mage— was the making of the seed of perfection called the philosopher's stone or the elixir of life. Formulas were inherited, debated, obfuscated, adulterated, encoded, translated and mistranslated into and out of a dozen different languages, but the basic schema remained the same. To effect what was called "the alchemical marriage," sulphur, the male element, and mercury, the female element, were fused in the crucible and this union generated the philosopher's stone, "the Royal Child" which, like Christ, redeemed all life to its highest form. H. D.'s spiritual challenge in *Trilogy* [hereafter referred to as *T*] is no less than the reawakening of this transmuting, projecting power: "the alchemist's key . . . / the elixir of life, the philosopher's stone" which "is yours if you surrender // sterile logic, trivial reason" (*T*).

Nearly every image in *Trilogy* enacts a transmutation meant to convince us of the universality of the process and to draw our perception along a continuous line from the poem's smallest event to its largest. These images are holograms or discrete cells of the poem containing in code the plan of the whole. The archetypal alchemical transformation, for example, the changing of lead to gold, reappears in a casually inserted icon as "corn . . . enclosed in black-lead, / ploughed land." Washed by earth's waters, heated by sun's fire, and strewn with seed, black-lead land becomes gold corn (*T*). "This is no rune nor riddle," H. D. reiterates; "it is happening everywhere" (*T*). In alchemical crucibles, under pressure, again and again, metamorphosis occurs: the mollusc shell holds a sand-grain, the egg-shell an egg; the heart-shell lodges a seed dropped by the phoenix; the cocoon houses a caterpillar, the shroud a worm preparing resurrection (*T*). Even the brain in its skull-case ferments and distills, dissolving sterile logic, generating new vision.

These images prepare our understanding of the poem's larger sweep. With properly cryptic encoding, the sections together retell the story of the making of the philosopher's stone. Each section contains a crucible, a purifying fire, and a double movement of destruction and creation; each moves us backward through time and inward across logic and custom, closer and closer to the culminating miracle of projection.

In "The Walls Do Not Fall," part one of *Trilogy*, the crucible is the city of London, flattened by ceaseless pounding, filled with the shards of civilization, flaming with "Apocryphal fire" (*T*). London's ruin makes it "the tomb, the temple" (*T*), a matrix of death and rebirth in which Old Testament wrath and vengeance yield to a higher form of being. In a dream-vision, H. D. witnesses the reborn god whom she calls "Ra, Osiris, *Amen*":

> he is the world-father,
> father of past aeons,
>
> present and future equally;
> beardless, not at all like Jehovah.
> (*The Walls Do Not Fall*)

This slender figure is the anointed son, the Christos, whose luminous amber eyes shine like transforming fire. With his entry into the poem, H. D. has half the alchemical formula, traditionally represented as the sun, fire, sulphur, the fathering principle.

In "Tribute to the Angels," part two of *Trilogy*, the crucible becomes the poem-bowl and the shards the word-fragments that survive as traces of the great traditions of female divinity. After proper invocations, with reverence for her materials and awe at the powers they hold, H. D. the poet-alchemist begins:

> Now polish the crucible
> and in the bowl distill
>
> a word most bitter, *marah*,
> a word bitterer still, *mar*,
>
> sea, brine, breaker, seducer,
> giver of life, giver of tears;
>
> Now polish the crucible
> and set the jet of flame
>
> under, till *marah-mar*
> are melted, fuse and join
>
> and change and alter,
> mer, mere, mère, mater, Maia, Mary,

Star of the Sea,
Mother.

(*Tribute to the Angels*)

This alchemical transaction creates a pulsing green-white, opalescent jewel which lives, breathes, and gives off "a vibration that we can not name" (*T*). After distilling, purifying, and refining this force, after witnessing intermediate manifestations and meditating on "the moon-cycle . . . the moon-shell" (*T*), H. D. has a dream-vision that closes this stage of her alchemy. It is an epiphany of the Lady, stripped of her myriad old forms—Isis, Astarte, Aset, Aphrodite, the old Eve, the Virgin Mary, "Our Lady of the Goldfinch, / Our Lady of the Candelabra" (*T*)—and released into new, as yet unnamed power. She is without the bridegroom, without the child; she is not hieratic; she is "no symbolic figure" (*T*). The book she carries "is not / the tome of the ancient wisdom" but "the unwritten volume of the new" (*T*). This as yet uninscribed essence is the renewed stuff of the other half of the alchemical formula, traditionally represented as the moon, mercury, the mothering principle.

In "The Flowering of the Rod," part three of *Trilogy,* the crucible is not a place or a poem but the legend of resurrection: "a tale of a Fisherman, / a tale of a jar or jars," an ancient story which in its Christian form is "the same—different—the same attributes, / different yet the same as before" (*T*). What the poet-alchemist must break down here is the familiar racist and misogynist reading of the Scriptures that dismisses Kaspar as a dark heathen and Mary Magdalene as a devil-ridden harlot, making both peripheral to the real story. In H. D.'s rewriting, they are central. The first two parts of *Trilogy* had precipitated a new male and female principle; now, in part three, they meet in alchemical marriage to effect the miraculous transformation. Kaspar, who might be Abraham or an Angel or even God (*T*), is here a somewhat forgetful and fallible philosopher, dream-interpreter, astrologer, and alchemist from a long line of Arabs who knew "the secret of the sacred processes of distillation" (*T*). He carries with him a sealed jar of myrrh exuding a fragrance that is the eternal essence "of all flowering things together" (*T*): the elixir of life, the seed of resurrection.

Kaspar was traveling to "a coronation and a funeral," like all alchemical transmutations "a double affair" (*T*), when found by Mary Magdalene, avatar of H. D.'s "mer, mere, mère, mater, Maia, Mary, // Star of the Sea, / Mother." When he momentarily abandons his patriarchal stiffness and, assuming a posture of reverence, stoops to pick up Mary's scarf, he is granted a vision that reaches back to "the islands of the Blest" and "the lost centre-island, Atlantis" (*T*) and forward to "the whole scope and plan // of our and his civilization on this, / his and our earth" (*T*). The spell he hears recovers the lost matriarchal genealogy, identifies Mary as heritor of *"Lilith born before Eve / and one born before Lilith, / and Eve"* (*T*, italics in original), and convinces Kaspar to yield her the precious myrrh. This act—in H. D.'s astonishing rewriting—seeds the resurrection. When Mary washes the feet of Christ, she anoints him with the elixir of life and insures that his crucifixion will be the first step in triumphant regeneration. Consecrated by Mary, Christ himself becomes the legendary philosopher's stone: the resurrection and the life.

Mary Magdalene's washing of the feet of Christ is the act of the alchemist: the projecting of the Mage's elixir onto substance prepared for transmutation. Behind the story of Kaspar and Mary is the old tale of sulphur and mercury; ahead of it is the work of the poet-alchemist who wanted to give us, through her combinations and recombinations of lost spells and legends, the power to transmute our own damaged civilization. The ultimate, audacious hope of *Trilogy* is that it might itself become an elixir of life, a resurrective power.

The mechanical philosophy that superseded alchemy posits a world of dead matter, matter without passion and without soul. This world of objects has often proved for its inhabitants a place of subjection, dejection, abjection, rejection—a place of energy twisted, repressed, or subverted. The nurturing universe H. D. glimpsed from the beginning of her career is profoundly different, a world of immanence and immediacy that could be called a projective universe. As the glow of radium with its puzzle of energy resident in matter led Marie Curie through her discoveries, the image of projection served as a conceptual and aesthetic focus for H. D.'s developing inquiries. An instrument of verbal organization and a source of intellectual and spiritual energies, projection was an act, an intuition, and an integration. It opened into, achieved, and helped to maintain the coherence and direction of her lifelong redemptive quest.

ALBERT GELPI

H. D.: Hilda in Egypt

H. D. always wrote her own personal and psychological dilemma against
and within the political turmoil of the twentieth century, the toils of love
enmeshed in the convulsions of war. Her marriage to and separation from
Richard Aldington turn on World War I, and that concatenation of private
and public trauma stands behind the Imagist poems of her first phase,
summed up in the *Collected Poems* of 1925. The sequences of *Trilogy*, written through the London blitzes of World War II, usher in the longer, multi-
valent, and more associative poems of her later years. But her last years were
to bring a third great burst of creativity. The travail of aging and illness did
not issue in the stoic silence which made Pound leave incomplete his life's
work in the *Cantos*, but instead, as with William Carlos Williams, made for
a final and climactic efflorescence of poetic expression. The results of this
third phase were *Helen in Egypt*, published in 1961 almost concurrently
with her death, and *Hermetic Definition*, published posthumously in 1972.

Even the reviewers who shied away from dealing with *Helen in Egypt*
as a poem by detaching particular lyrics for dutiful praise (as though they
were still Imagist pieces) recognized dimly that *Helen* was the culmination
of a life in poetry. But it is an event even more culturally signal than that:
it is the most ambitious and successful long poem ever written by a woman
poet, certainly in English. It is so often observed as to take on a kind of

From *Coming to Light: American Women Poets in the Twentieth Century,* edited by
Diane Wood Middlebrook and Marilyn Yalom. © 1985 by Albert Gelpi. The University of Michigan Press, 1985.

fatality that no woman has ever written an epic, that women poets seem constrained to the minor note and the confabulations of the heart. H. D. confounds that complacent dictum by assuming and redefining the grounds of the epic. Early on the poem asks

> Is Fate inexorable?
> does Zeus decree that, forever,
> Love should be born of War?

The *Iliad* showed War born of Love, but H. D. repossessed the Trojan materials that have inspired the Western epic from Homer to Pound and converted them into an anti-epic centered less on heroes like Achilles and Hector than on a heroine, none other than the fabulous woman who, male poets have told us, roused men to Love, and so to War.

Many of the masterworks of American writing—*Walden* and *Moby-Dick* and *Absalom, Absalom!, Leaves of Grass* and *The Cantos, Four Quartets* and *Paterson*—are *sui generis*. They make their idiosyncratic statements in their own unique form. So *Helen in Egypt* draws Greek and Egyptian myths, epic and psychoanalysis and occult gnosticism into an "odyssey" of consciousness played out as a series of lyrics written in irregular free verse tercets of varying length, linked by prose commentaries sometimes longer than the lyrics. The poem is divided into books, eight lyrics to a book, seven books to Part I, "Pallinode," and to Part II, "Leuké," and six to the concluding part, "Eidolon." "Pallinode" was written at Lugano in the summer of 1952; "Leuké," the next year at the Küsnacht Klinik near Zurich, H. D.'s base of residence after 1953; and "Eidolon" again at Lugano during the summer of 1954. H. D. came to think of the poem as a trilogy, and the narrative too is laid out in a number of interrelated triangles. The speakers in "Pallinode," which takes place in an Egyptian temple near the coast after the war, are Helen, who was rumored to have spent the war there rather than at Troy, and Achilles, the Trojan nemesis lost at sea and shipwrecked in Egypt; the speakers in Part II are Helen and her old lover Paris on Leuké, *l'isle blanche*, and then Helen and Theseus, her old benefactor and counselor in Athens; the triad of voices in "Eidolon" are Helen and Paris and Achilles. Through the other male voices Helen's is, of course, not only the point of view but the subsuming consciousness. And Helen is, of course, H. D.'s persona.

A notebook entry in 1955 observed: "I had found myself, I had found my alter-ego or my double—and that my mother's name was Helen has no doubt something to do with it." And the configuration of male characters around Helen recreates fantasized versions of her governing relationships with men as she strove, now on an epic scale, to lift "the tragic events and sordid realities of *my* life" into myth.

Theseus is the easiest to designate. Most readers have recognized in him an image of Sigmund Freud. He served H. D. during the thirties and after as wise old man, surrounded in his study by ancient Greek figurines, as he applied reason to help her sort out the confusion of her life and feelings. Like Freud for H. D., Theseus is for Helen the wise, paternal authority who offers his couch to her for rest and an analytic rehearsal of her amatory embroilments.

The associations with Paris and with Achilles are more important and elusive because less fixed and more inclusive; they span all H. D.'s adult life up to the time of her writing of the poem. As for Paris, her involvement with Dr. Eric Heydt, her doctor and analyst at Küsnacht Klinik, had almost immediately passed from the professional into the personal and romantic despite the fact that she was decades older than he, and in a notebook she confessed that the complications of the relationship extended the poem into its second part and specifically led to the introduction of Paris. But behind Heydt stood Pound: in *HERmione* she saw the young Pound as "Paris with the apple," saw his luxuriant red hair as "the Phrygian Cap of Paris." He called her his "Dryad," and so she signed her letters to him to the end of her life. He wrote his famous invocation "A Tree" to her in the "Hilda Book" during their courtship, and *HERmione* echoes her acceptance. "I am a tree. TREE is my new name out of the Revelations." And now years later Paris calls Helen "Dendritis, . . . Helena of the trees."

In the "Compassionate Friendship" notebook (which also dates from the mid-1950s), H. D. rehearsed "the sequence of my initiators" throughout her life: Pound; Aldington; from the London days of World War I John Cournos and D. H. Lawrence and Cecil Grey (the father of her daughter Perdita); Bryher's second husband Kenneth MacPherson (who had been H. D.'s lover); Walther Schmideberg, her analyst and close friend during the time of the final divorce decree from Aldington in 1938; and now Eric Heydt as the "inheritor" of the long male line of initiators. In much the same way the figure of Paris summed up all the men in her life, from Pound to Heydt, including Aldington.

Moreover, she particularly associated Heydt with Pound. When Heydt gave her an injection at perhaps their initial encounter at the Klinik, he transfixed her with the question "You know Ezra Pound, don't you?" "This was a shock coming from a stranger," she told her journal. "Perhaps he injected me or re-injected me with Ezra." The sexual image is appropriate enough; Heydt persisted in pressing her about her relationship with her first lover, and once even asked her—to her distaste—whether the relationship had been sexual. The Pound memoir, *End to Torment*, H. D. wrote in 1958 only after repeated urging from Heydt that she recover her memories of the young man who had loved her and confirmed her a poet. Testimony that Pound was a living presence in her mind extends beyond *End to Torment* to the separate Helen sequence "Winter Love," written in 1959 and published in *Hermetic Definition,* in which Helen/Hilda relives her early love for "Odysseus." So she incorporated into the Paris of her *Helen,* she said, an imaginative presence or medium who stood behind Heydt and was associated with "the history of poor Ezra and my connection with him."

The figure of Achilles is composite in much the same way as Paris. Notebook entries specifically connect him with Lord Hugh Dowding, the Air Marshal of the Battle of Britain with whom H. D. shared spiritualist experiences and for whom she served briefly as medium. Though she saw Dowding only at two lectures about his communications with lost RAF pilots and at seven meetings, she felt a spiritual affinity for him that was like an "engagement." She was shattered when he broke off their acquaintance, and "in 1952, after I knew of the Air Marshall's [sic] marriage (Sept. 1951), I wrote the first section of the *Helen* sequence." The rupture released creative energy to cope with the situation, as had the separation from Aldington earlier.

> We had come together through and for the messages. There was a feeling of exaltation in my later discovery, it was not I, personally, who was repudiated. An "engagement" was broken, but broken on a new level. . . . My life was enriched, my creative energy was almost abnormal. I wrote the *Avon,* I wrote three "works" (unpublished) on my unparalleled experiences. I wrote the long *Helen* sequence.

But Achilles was associated with other figures as well. Dowding reminded her of her father in some ways: "I know *ad astra,* my father's profession, the iridescent moons he shows us. I know *ad astra,* the Air Marshall's profession. I know the wide-faring, hypnotic, rather mad grey eyes of both of them." In another notebook she recounts a dream in which her older brother Gilbert (for whom she felt such love and such competition for her mother's love) is strangling her, and associates the dream with the episode in which Achilles tries to strangle Helen. But more importantly, just as Pound stands behind Heydt in Paris, so Aldington stands behind Dowding in Achilles. Paris's and Achilles' initials are as significant as Helen's. And where Paris represents the line of initiators in H. D.'s life who in one way and another carried her away, Achilles represents specifically the rough and devastating threat of the masculine, not unrelated to the romantic Paris-aspect, but specifically that aspect of the masculine which cast her off and cast her down. The poem enacts Helen's apotheosis as she transcends Paris's power over her and transforms Achilles' rejection into a divine marriage, a *conjunctio oppositorum* ordained by the gods.

"Is Fate inexorable? / does Zeus decree that, forever, / Love should be born of War?" The poem finally answers *yes:* divine decree requires that we submit ourselves to life, for all the war wounds and mortal blows, so that, providentially, in comprehending the train of temporal events, we can accept and transcend them; participation in the design decreed for time at last earns identity. *Helen in Egypt* is, then, H. D.'s death song which is at once a capitulation to and a reconstitution of life.

Helen's union with Achilles is posited from the start. She tells his lost companions:

> God for his own purpose
> wills it so, that I
>
> stricken, forsaken draw to me,
> through magic greater than the trial of arms,
> your own invincible, unchallenged Sire.

Paris and Theseus will play their parts; but everything contributes, however unwittingly, to the foreordained syzygy of Helen and Achilles. And God's emissary and instigator is the mother-goddess of the sea Thetis. Thetis it was who had unintentionally precipitated the war by failing to invite Eris (Strife) along with the other gods to the banquet for her marriage to Peleus. Excluded from the celebration of Eros, Eris sowed the discord which ended in the Trojan conflict, and the death of Achilles, son of Thetis and Peleus. Eris was devious in her revenge; she tossed a golden apple marked "for the fairest" into the banquet hall and when Hera, Athene, and Aphrodite began to wrangle for it, Zeus ordered that the quarrel be settled by the judgment of Paris, the youthful shepherd-son of the Trojan king. Aphrodite won the apple by promising Paris the most beautiful woman in the world, who turned out to be Helen, Menelaus's queen. Thetis had counterschemes to thwart Eris's vengeance and save her son: she sought immortality for her son by dipping him into the river Styx, she charged Chiron with tutoring him in peaceful pursuits, she settled him into a safe, remote marriage with the daughter of the king of Scyros. All in vain: Achilles left that haven with Patroclus to fight before the walls of Troy and to take various women as his sexual prize, only to meet his death; with Greek victory at hand under Achilles' leadership, the vengeful Paris slew Achilles with an arrow shot into the heel Thetis had held when the Stygian waters rendered Achilles otherwise invulnerable.

All this background is sketched in through flashbacks and memories, but the poem begins with the dramatic encounter between Helen and Achilles. Dead and past the "fire of battle" and the "fire of desire," he is ferried to Egypt, an alien shore where he does not recognize as the dread Helen the woman brooding on the hieroglyphs in the temple of Amen. From the time when Helen's glance from the Trojan ramparts had locked with his below on the plains, his fate was set. They had moved, all unknowing, to this meeting, and Thetis is the link and catalyst: "How did we know each other? / was it the sea-enchantment in his eyes of Thetis his sea-mother?" When Achilles grieves with a boy's petulant outrage at suffering the mortal fate of a mere man, Helen prays to comfort him like a mother:

> *let me love him, as Thetis, his mother,*
> for I knew him, I saw in his eyes
> the sea-enchantment, but he

> knew not yet Helen of Sparta,
> knew not Helen of Troy,
> knew not Helen, hated of Greece.

When he does recognize her, he "clutched my throat / with his fingers' remorseless steel," but Helen's plea to Thetis relaxed his grip. The last book of "Pallinode" presents Thetis speaking now "in complete harmony with Helen." For Thetis becomes Helen's mother too—her surrogate mother, adopted by the mutually consenting love of "mother" and "daughter"; Thetis is the biographical Helen, and the fictional Helen is Hilda.

From her mother Helen, Hilda felt that she drew her poetic and religious capabilities, her affinity with the power of the word and the Word. But that Helen gave Hilda no maternal confirmation or blessing, she seemed to prefer her brother Gilbert. Even before she brought the problem to Freud in the thirties, H. D. stated her disappointment in *HERmione*. There the daughter resents her mother, a failed artist conforming to patriarchal norms, because she has "no midwife power," "can't lift me out of" her thwarted inarticulateness; and yet "one should sing hymns of worship to her, powerful, powerless, all-powerful. . . ." *Trilogy* and, even more strongly, *Helen* are the hymns she could not sing in *HERmione*. For in the *Helen* poem Hilda assumes her mother's name at last, and the word she is given by Thetis to speak to her murderous son is Thetis's own name, the mother-name. With that word aggressor becomes brother, hetaira becomes sister, mother embraces daughter with son; with that name Helen and Achilles are reconciled as lovers and siblings.

So complete is the mother's harmony with the filial Helen at the climax of "Pallinode" that she acts as psychopomp revealing Helen's selfhood, to be achieved under her aegis. Thetis's lyric rune inaugurates Helen's initiation into arcane female mysteries, drawn from the deeps of nature and of the psyche:

> A woman's wiles are a net;
> they would take the stars
> or a grasshopper in its mesh;
>
> they would sweep the sea
> for a bubble's iridescence
> or a flying-fish;
>
> they would plunge beneath the surface,
> without fear of the treacherous deep
> or a monstrous octopus;
>
> what unexpected treasure,
> what talisman or magic ring
> may the net find?
>
> frailer than spider spins,
> or a worm for its bier,
> deep as a lion or a fox
>
> or a panther's lair,
> leaf upon leaf, hair upon hair
> as a bird's nest,
>
> Phoenix
> has vanquished
> that ancient enemy, Sphinx.

Thetis's unriddling of the temple hieroglyphs reveals Helen's name rising from the rubble of war:

> The Lords have passed a decree,
> the Lords of the Hierarchy,
> that Helen be worshipped,

be offered incense
upon the altars of Greece,
with her brothers, the Dioscuri;

from Argos, from distant Scythia,
from Delos, from Arcady,
the harp-strings will answer

the chant, the rhythm, the metre,
the syllables H-E-L-E-N-A;
Helena, reads the decree,

shall be shrined forever;
in Melos, in Thessaly,
they shall honour the name of Love,

begot of the Ships and of War;
one indestructible name,
to inspire the Scribe and refute

the doubts of the dissolute;
this is the Law,
this, the Mandate:

let no man strive against Fate,
Helena has withstood
the rancour of time and of hate.

Thetis goes on to distinguish Helen's fate from that of her twin sister
Clytemnestra, for Clytemnestra's relation to the masculine has been destructive and self-destructive. As Helen's "shadow" Clytemnestra has obscured
her sister's quest for identity, but now Thetis directs Helen to self-discovery
through a creative connection with the masculine. Helen shall be immortal-
ized with her twin brothers the Dioscuri. The decree of Amen-Thoth,
"Nameless-of-many-Names," is

that *Helena* shall remain
one name, inseparable
from the names of the Dioscuri,

who are not two but many,
as you read the writing, the script,
the thousand-petalled lily.

And the union with the brothers is concurrent with, or consequent to, the divine decree that "Helena / be joined to Achilles." The hieroglyphs have sealed Helen's destiny, but the periplum to Achilles is a circumnavigation, first to Paris on the white isle of Leuké and then to Theseus in Athens to find the future by sorting out the past.

Why Leuké, *l'isle blanche*? "Because," the prose commentary says, "here, Achilles is said to have married Helen who bore him a son, Euphorion." The import of this remark will become clear later, but at the present it seems misleading since the first three books of "Leuké" narrate the re-encounter between Paris and his *Dendritis, . . . Helena of the trees.*" Paris calls them "Adonis and Cytheraea," associating Helen with his goddess Aphrodite, and seeks to rouse her from Egyptian secrets and Greek intellection to rekindled sexual passion: "O Helena, tangled in thought, / be Rhodes' Helena, *Dendritis,* / why remember Achilles?"; "I say he never loved you." Paris harkens back to a life of passion on the old terms, now to Helen past feeling and past recall.

Helen flees Paris's importuning to seek the sage counsel of the aged Theseus, who wraps her in the security of warm blankets on his couch, like a swaddled baby or cocooned butterfly. At first Theseus counters her recoil from "Paris as Eros-Adonis" with Athenian reasonableness, urging happiness with Paris and denouncing Achilles as a choice of death over life: "even a Spirit loves laughter / did you laugh with Achilles? No"; "you found life here with Paris. . . ." Why should she choose to "flame out, incandescent" in death with Achilles, who has exploited women all his life? Nevertheless, though Theseus may not want to admit it, Helen is no longer Dendritis, and Achilles may not be his old self either. In any case, Paris seems too fevered and puerile to be the one she seeks.

Theseus comes to see that she longs for a new and perfect lover "beyond Trojan and Greek"; she is the Phoenix ready to rise from the ashes, the butterfly cracking the chrysalis and "wavering / like a Psyche / with half-dried wings." Though Theseus sees Helen's development and stops pleading for Paris, he tries importuning for himself. He had been captivated by Helen since she was a girl, and H. D. may have had in mind Freud's angry complaint during a therapeutic session that his pupil found him too old to love when she had Theseus offer to serve Helen as someone "half-way" to her ideal Lover. The suggestion is tender and touching—but out of the question. As with Freud and H. D., Theseus becomes Helen's "god-father" by bringing her to a wisdom which essentially differs from his own. His response requires her to clarify her own and prepares her to leave him behind as well as Paris in order to seek out Achilles once and for all. As for old transgressions,

Achilles and she are "past caring"; the future need not be blocked by the past, life can lead only to afterlife.

Paris's adolescent eroticism makes him seem her own child, perhaps even Achilles' son—in fact, "incarnate / Helen-Achilles," so that, in an inversion of chronological time, "he, my first lover, was created by my last. . . ." On one level this line may recall again the special connection between Pound and Heydt in the sequence of male initiators, and the reappearance of Pound as a potent psychological presence during these late years in part through the agency of Heydt. But a more relevant reading of the line would see Helen as setting aside as outdated and outgrown all the lovers and initiators of her previous life for a new kind of love to be found with Achilles. When the prose commentary at the beginning of part 2 said that on Leuké "Achilles is said to have married Helen who bore him a son," the statement seemed erroneous or misleading, for Helen met not Achilles but Paris. But, as it turns out, her refusal to turn back the life cycle makes Paris seem, regressively, a child to her. Through Theseus she reconstitutes herself, reclaiming her past with a new maturity. And so by a kind of backward illogic the recognition of Paris as child confirms Achilles as husband-father in her heightened consciousness.

For in this poem Achilles and Paris matter only in relation to and in definition of Helen. The central insight which opens the resolution of the poem is the realization that she is the Phoenix, the Psyche self-born:

> beyond all other, the Child,
> the child in the father,
> the child in the mother,
>
> the child-mother, yourself.

Helen enwombs the entire process; the "child-mother" bears herself. When Helen asks in the next lyric how the masculine dualities—her twin brothers Castor and Pollux, Achilles and Theseus—can be reconciled, the wise old Theseus answers that the polarities meet in herself. His words carry him past Greek common sense into ecstatic vision, the sound-echoes and rhythms of the words rocking the lines to a hallucinated resolution beyond words. His incantation, at once limpid and opaque, veiling the revelation in the act of revealing the veiled secret, brings "Leuké" to a climax:

> Thus, thus, thus,
> as day, night,
> as wrong, right,

as dark, light,
as water, fire,
as earth, air,

as storm, calm,
as fruit, flower,
as life, death,

as death, life;
the rose deflowered,
the rose re-born;

Helen in Egypt,
Helen at home,
Helen in Hellas forever.

The prose commentary informs us that "Helen understands, though we do not know exactly what it is that she understands," but the interplay of opposites in a transcendent pattern (which Emerson called the cosmic law of Compensation) is now to her "very simple." Reconciled "to Hellas forever," she sets out to return to Achilles in Egypt for the long-appointed union; Theseus has no choice but to bless her voyage to "Dis, Hades, Achilles." Her fate is not her dead life with Paris, but renewal with the dead Achilles; her myth is not Venus and Adonis, as Paris urged, but Persephone and Hades. And the hierogamy will be personal and psychological: "I will encompass the infinite / in time, in the crystal, / in my thought here."

Early in part 3, "Eidolon," Paris abandons his recriminations against Pluto-Achilles ("his is a death-cult"), and accepts him as father with Helen replacing Hecuba as mother. Now the poem circles back with deeper comprehension to the meeting with which it began, when Achilles, raging against his mortality, attacks Helen, until his mother's—Helen's god-mother's—intervention relaxes his death-grip into an embrace. Achilles had forsaken his mother when he went to war; only after ten years on the Trojan plains did he promise to return to her if she helped him seize victory. But with triumph in his grasp, he suffered his human destiny. Paris's arrow found Achilles' heel, and he returned to his mother in a strange land, finding her in the eyes and person of Helen. With Paris reclaimed as son, Helen reaches her apotheosis as mother. Now we understand more clearly than in Book 1 why the single word "Thetis," gasped in Achilles' strangle-grasp, metamorphoses Helen in his eyes into a sea-goddess. For that mother-name

would weld him to her
who spoke it, who thought it,

who stared through the fire,
who stood as if to withstand
the onslaught of fury and battle,

who stood unwavering but made
as if to dive down, unbroken,
undefeated in the tempest roar

and thunder, inviting mountains
of snow-clad foam-tipped
green walls of sea-water

to rise like ramparts about her,
walls to protect yet walls to dive under,
dive through and dive over.

The two "will always" for that "eternal moment" comprise a syzygy of
L'Amour, La Mort: "this is Love, this is Death, / this is my last Lover."
Paris, discarded as lover, is reborn as their child, and the offspring of their
syzygy is not just Paris, but themselves restored: Achilles "the child in Chiron's care," Helen the maiden at Theseus's knee. The mythic psychological
status which Helen attains in the poem encompasses mother and wife and
restored daughter: Demeter-Persephone-Kore in one. In writing her own Hel-
en-text, H. D. arrived at a reading of identity which resumed and surpassed
the past. That moment—between time and eternity and participating in
both—is the "final illumination" of the poem, and it is the moment of death.
Through the mother-goddess she has conceived and come full term, dying
and rising to herself. That metamorphosis, spelled out in the poem, has sealed
her life cycle in the eternal pattern. "Sealed" in several senses: it brings her
life to fulfillment and conclusion, it impresses on that life its distinctive signet
or hieroglyph, and it affirms that life with irrevocable authority. Helen had
said: "to me, the wheel is a seal . . . / the wheel is still." Under the name of
Helen, H. D. spelled out her hermetic definition. Though *Helen in Egypt* is
a death-hymn, H. D. told her notebook: "I am alive in the *Helen* sequence"
because "there I had found myself"; those poems "give me everything."

Early in the poem Helen asks: "is it only the true immortals / who partake of mortality?" The poem's response inverts the proposition: true par-
takers of mortality achieve immortality. The moment of death is the moment
of gnosis, in which life and consciousness conclude and transcend themselves;
Helen becomes, with Achilles, a "New Mortal"—L'Amour/La Mort in a
higher configuration. This is what the last lyric of Book 3 postulates in lines
whose declarative simplicity does not designate the mystery they bespeak.

Paris before Egypt, Paris after,
is Eros, even as Thetis,
the sea-mother, is Paphos;

so the dart of Love
is the dart of Death,
and the secret is no secret;

the simple path
refutes at last
the threat of the Labyrinth,

the Sphinx is seen,
the Beast is slain
and the Phoenix-nest

reveals the innermost
key or the clue to the rest
of the mystery;

there is no before and no after,
there is one finite moment
that no infinite joy can disperse

or thought of past happiness
tempt from or dissipate;
now I know the best and the worst;

the seasons revolve around
a pause in the infinite rhythm
of the heart and of heaven.

To some readers the "final illumination" to which *Helen in Egypt* builds
will seem gnomic, perhaps nonsensical. But the vision of the eternal moment,
with time concentered individually and cosmically in eternity, is H. D.'s
occult version of Eliot's Christian "still point of the turning world." In fact,
the conclusion of *Helen in Egypt* deserves to be set beside such exalted
moments in poems of old age as Eliot's in the *Quartets*, when "the fire and
the rose are one." Or Frost's arrival in "Directive" back at the spring-source
which is his watering place ("Drink and be whole again"). Or Williams's
declaration through his dead "Sparrow": "This was I, / a sparrow. I did my
best; / farewell." Or Pound's conclusion to *The Cantos:* "Do not move. / Let
the wind speak. / That is Paradise"; or his version of Herakles' expiring
words:

what

SPLENDOUR,

IT ALL COHERES.

Different in tone and perspective as these moments are, the reader either is or is not already there with the poet. By this point, in the particular poem and in the evolution of the poet's life's work, evocation has become invocation; image and symbol, bare statement. Further demonstration is out of the question.

Where Frost's final sense of things remained skeptical and Williams's naturalistic, H. D.'s was like Eliot's religious, and like Pound's heterodoxly so. No resume or excerpting of passages can indicate how subtly the images and leitmotifs of *Helen in Egypt* are woven into the design. Some reviewers found the prose passages distracting intrusions among the lyrics, but H. D. wanted, like the other poets I have cited, a counterpoint of lyric expression and reflective commentary. In identification with the mother-goddess, assimilating Greek and Egyptian, Christian and gnostic wisdom, H. D. came to read the scribble of her life as hieroglyph. Nothing need be forgotten; nothing could be denied; everything was caught up in the resolution.

The summons of Thetis the sea-mother which closes part 1, "Helen—come home," initiates a refrain that echoes throughout the poem and receives a gloss in a notebook entry: "We say (old-fashioned people used to say) when someone dies, he or she has *gone home*. I was looking for home, I think. But a sort of heaven-is-my-home. . . ." The recovery of the human mother as goddess, the discovery of the mother in herself and herself in the mother constituted "heaven-is-my-home," and allowed, in the concluding lyric, a return of the lover-twin of Helen-Achilles to the mother-sea.

> *But what could Paris know of the sea,*
> *its beat and long reverberation,*
> *its booming and delicate echo,*
>
> *its ripple that spells a charm*
> *on the sand, the rock-lichen,*
> *the sea-moss, the sand,*
>
> *and again and again, the sand;*
> *what does Paris know of the hill and hollow*
> *of billows, the sea-road?*
>
> *what could he know of the ships*
> *from his Idaean home,*
> *the crash and spray of the foam,*

> *the wind, the shoal, the broken shale,*
> *the infinite loneliness*
> *when one is never alone?*
>
> *only Achilles could break his heart*
> *and the world for a token,*
> *a memory forgotten.*

As the poem indicates, Helen's recovery of the mother coincides with a shift in her relation to the masculine, away from the dominating Paris, who used to have power over her, to a new Achilles as filial-fraternal partner, and the shift signals a reimagining of the central theme of H. D.'s fiction and verse.

The biographical source of the sexual anxiety is clear: the broken engagement to Pound, the broken marriage to Aldington in the years during and immediately after the war. But she continued to seek the reconciliation that would heal the psychic wounds. Her correspondence with John Cournos, a member of their London circle, shows her intense concern about Aldington before, during, even after the separation. As late as February 1929, she wanted to scotch any rumor Cournos had heard of a "final quarrel" with Aldington, and in July she sent Cournos this excited word:

> without any intervention R. wrote me and I have been in close touch with him ever since. . . . We saw one another much in Paris and write constantly. We are very, very close to one another intellectually and spiritually. There may be some definite separation later, but if there is, it will be because of FRIENDLINESS and nothing else. There is no question of R. and self ever becoming in any way "intimate" again and that is why this other relationship is so exquisite and sustaining.

In fact, as she might well have known, she was never to reach "this other relationship"—intellectual and spiritual without the compulsions and vulnerabilities of the physical—with Aldington, but even their divorce in 1938 did not break off communication between them. They went their separate, and often stormy, ways; but during the years at Küsnacht Klinik they were still corresponding, and Dr. Heydt was as curious about Aldington as he was about Pound.

It is clear that after she fell from the innocence of that first love with Pound into the betrayals and counterbetrayals of sexual relationships, she often asked herself "Why had I ever come down out of that tree?" By the time Achilles succeeds Paris at the end of *Helen,* those male characters have archetypal functions within the design of female consciousness which the poem formulates. H. D. saw the whole succession of initiators, including Dr. Heydt, in Pound, and she also saw in Achilles, as she told her notebook, the "héros fatale" who had failed her repeatedly—from Pound and Aldington down to the "Lord Howell" (Dowding) of the unpublished World War II novels and now Heydt at the Klinik. Yet since the "héros fatale" held the key to her self-fulfillment, she must imagine the terms on which Helen would marry Achilles. An Achilles who had undergone a sea-change: the Aldington she lost early in her marriage, possessed once and for all in the consanguinity of the mother. The mother gave her the word and the word was her own name: Hilda's Helen poem. There, in the imagined possibilities of the word, she attained at last after great cost the "exquisite and sustaining" relationship she could never establish in life.

More especially so, since the union resolved the parental as well as sexual crisis. In a notebook passage, quoted above, which notes the association of her astronomer father with the airman Dowding in the figure of Achilles, H. D. notes again the association of Helen with her mother. The passage then continues: "in the sequence, Helen is ideally or poetically or epically 'married' to Achilles. . . . I know the father, the mother, and the third of the trio or trilogy, the poem, the creation, the thing they begot or conceived between them. It is all perfect." The creation of the poem has brought Helen to perfection as mother-daughter-wife: the completed feminine archetype. In the ideal-poetic-epic marriage of Helen to Achilles H. D. attains "the final and complete solution of the life-long search for the answer—the companion in-time and out-of-time together." In the poem Achilles is Helen's "Achilles" now, father-husband-son, and together they consign themselves to the sea.

The perfect union of Helen and Achilles is therefore a death marriage, as in the "marriage" poems of Emily Dickinson, realized in the imaginative creation. If Dickinson's "love" poetry remains more indirect and inhibited than *Helen in Egypt,* the cause may lie in part in Dickinson's attachment to her stern father: a bonding so strong that it kept her from the experience of the wife and the mother; she knew the masculine as the virgin-daughter, at the furthest extreme as virgin-bride: Kore rather than Persephone or Demeter. H. D's Helen would not be daughter to Theseus or hetaira to Paris; through Thetis she made Achilles her own, husband and father and son as she was wife and mother and daughter. Helen Doolittle was the source of Hilda's visionary power over the word, and in her Helen-poem Hilda formulated her hermetic definition.

The scope of that vision also made for another notable difference be-

tween *Helen in Egypt* and Dickinson's love poems. Wrenching and exhilarating as they are, Dickinson's love poems remain a collection of individual
pieces at cross-purposes, recording ambivalences that kept her the father's
virgin daughter. In the long, tortuous, fragmented history of women writing
about their womanhood, the supreme distinction of *Helen in Egypt,* with all
its idiosyncrasies, is that it transforms the male war epic into the woman's
love lyric sustained at a peak of intensity for an epic's length, and the woman's myth it evolves posits the supremacy of the mother: Helen self-born in
Thetis, Hilda self-born in Helen.

ROBERT DUNCAN

The H. D. Book: *Part 2, Chapter 6*

S eptember 2, 1964

In the current issue of the poets' journal *Open Space,* I find in an untitled
poem by Harold Dull upon listening to the opera *Orfeo* the concept that in
each step of the life drama of Orpheus he gains a question: "and by the
time / he goes into the dark / to lose her the second time . . .

> he has as many apparently forever to be unanswered questions as
> there are strings on his lyre"

striking a chord with those passages of H. D.'s *Helen in Egypt* where in part
2 of the "Eidolon" section it seems that Helen in her living has gained "a
rhythm as yet unheard," and that history—the war at Troy and Troy's fall
are "Apollo's snare / so that poets forever / should be caught in the maze of
the Walls / of a Troy that never fell."

"Was it a question asked / to which there was no answer?" H. D. asks,
and then:

> who lured the players from home
> or imprisoned them in the Walls,
>
> to inspire us with endless,
> intricate questioning?

So the proposition of the last poem in "Eidolon," part 2, states: "*There is*

From *The Southern Review* 21, no. 1 (January 1985). © 1985 by Robert Duncan.

only a song now and rhetorical questions that have already been answered."
But the rhetorical question, it has already been answered in the poem, is
meant not to find its answer but to incite the movement of the poem, leads
on, opening a way for the flow of the poetic feeling to go, question and
answer for the sake of a rhythm; as the questions of high and low, of the
gap in society or consciousness or concept, of the proposition taken up from
William James's *Principles of Psychology* of many realities entering into the
picture of the total world of man's experience, or the idea of a Permission
or Grace given, are instrumental and will be seen at last to be as many as
the strings of the lyre to which they belong upon which I play. The lyre in
turn existing for the sake of the book I am making here, drawing from the
faces of Pound, Williams, H. D., the faces of the book's Pound, Williams,
H. D., or from the face of the Permission Itself, the face that appears in the
drawing, belonging to the work we are about, you with me, if you follow.
"There is a spell, for instance," the Poet has told us in the beginning, "in
every sea-shell," that given life we make it a life of our own, and that that
lasts—the potsherd, the ghostly outlines of Mohenjodaro's city plan, the
song of Troy—when the life and the men are lost. Back, back, back we must
go to find sufficient self to live in to these beings, taking being.

For I needed this book for a place for her to exist in me. "The fate of
modern poetry as a whole," Burkhardt wrote a century ago in *The Three
Powers,* "is the consciousness, born of the history of literature, of its relationship to the poetry of *all* times and peoples. On that background, it
appears as an imitation or echo." By imitation or echo alone then, if they
alone are possible. Searching whatever text mind or heart recalled, argument
or the beginning of a rhythm, to find out an H. D., the H. D. this book
means to unfold. A rhetorical question, to give rise, as the pencil draws, as
the brush paints, to a figure of many faces known and yet to be known. The
lady has her own life. She is not now Hilda Doolittle, and only in her special
sense is she the poetess H. D.—she is the person who narrates her story in
The War Trilogy and she has just that one poem in which to exist; as Claribel
of H. D.'s poem *Good Frend* is given the poem in which to have a life, to
be a person of the drama. She is not in the *Dramatis Personae* of Shakespeare's *The Tempest,* where she is named only in passing "*the king's fair
daughter Claribel*"

> And we read later, *in one voyage*
> *Did Claribel her husband find at Tunis:*
>
> Claribel was outside all of this
> *The Tempest* came after they left her;
> Read for yourself, *Dramatis Personae*

. . . .
Read through again, *Dramatis Personae;*
She is not there at all, but Claribel,
Claribel, the birds shrill, Claribel,
Claribel echoes from this rainbow-shell
I stooped just now to gather from the sand—

has just that poem *Good Frend* in which to exist in the heart of H. D., taken over from Shakespeare. Go read through the *War Trilogy;* you will see how I have taken up what would furnish my even blind will as I work with its substance. As if I were a gap, making up my self. A critical study? There may be times when the painter sees his own insight in a passage of his painting and he had then to look deeper until he saw what otherwise might have been his insight as the work's factor. And passages of fine writing, bravura, might come in, only to be obliterated in the trying, painstaking drawing out of a task he knew no other way to do, or kept once he had taken that way, like the under drawing showing through in Picasso's *Guernica* that reminds us it is to participate in the idea that we work, line over line as in the first drawings we recall in the cave's depths, and so in faith— his one faith—in the saving grace of his being involved in the Work itself, and having this work given—as if in love giving himself over to the Work— in the (unknown) creative will that drives all speech, all writing, all language he believes . . .

You know the poem, you have read it well. I do not feel you do justice to the *War Trilogy* yet, you write; for you as a friend (a reader) of the original know it is so much more, so much other than the likeness I have drawn. Or you, who have never loved (read) the original, tell me that I make too much of a poor matter, the passages of the poem that appear never come up to the poem I am imagining. The lady smiles at us, for this figure I am drawing from of the Lady with a Book may be the very lady who appears in her *Tribute to the Angels,* her author in my author,

which is no easy trick, difficult
even for the experienced stranger

H. D. tells us. Is she talking about this Person's relating Herself to time here, in the rhythm of the clock's ticking, to appear to the poet in her dream? But it is a double image, for the Lady appears to the reader as She appeared to the writer in the medium of the poem, another trick, in the hypnotic measure, the evocative tick of syllables in procession. She is so communicated.

My other reader who is not H. D.'s reader, who does not get what I draw from or, unsympathetic, sees only in a bad light or a poor light—what can be known of my own sense in working of how little I get it, how blurred often the work is, yet, for I have been working here over four years, having always the source of the original that does not go dead on me, that gives again and again, of what a life there is in this for me, keeping the nexus of what she means to me working in the imagination.

> I see her as you project her
> not out of place

the reader or critic with goodwill addresses the artist in *Tribute to the Angels*

> you have done very well by her
> (to repeat your own phrase)
>
> you have carved her tall and unmistakable,
> a hieratic figure, the veiled Goddess

"O yes—you understand," the poet replies:

> but she wasn't hieratic, she wasn't frozen,
> she wasn't very tall.

She was demented surely. Though analysis may read unconscious sexual content in poems, only in the early erotic masque *Hymen* with its "dark purple" color have I found overt reference to sexuality, heat and snow of maiden chastity, and then in the tradition of the true nuptial rite a recounting of what happens in the taking of the flower of the bride's vagina:

> There with his honey-seeking lips
> The bee clings close and warmly sips,
> And seeks with honey-thighs to sway
> And drink the very flower away.
>
> (Ah, stern the petals drawing back;
> Ah, rare, ah, virginal her breath!)
>
> Crimson, with honey-seeking lips
> The sun lies hot across his back
> The gold is flecked across his wings.
> Quivering he sways and quivering clings
> (Ah, rare her shoulders drawing back!)
> One moment, then the plunderer slips
> Between the purple flower lips.

These images clothe but to enhance the sexual lure. But throughout her work she bears testimony to a fever that is not localized, the heat of *Mid-Day,* and a fierce yearning that can be avid, a sensuality that can declare, as in *Red Roses for Bronze:*

> sensing underneath the garment seam
> ripple and flash and gleam
> of indrawn muscle
> and of those more taut,
> I feel that I must turn and tear and rip
> the fine cloth
> from this moulded thigh and hip,
> force you to grasp my soul's sincerity.

The clothing postpones, incites and increases the craving the sexual organ itself will exorcise. The question that calls up not an answer but an increased rhetoric or current, the freefloating desire, takes over. In the prose work *Nights,* written in the 1930s, Natalia Saunderson seeks this excitement in itself in making love; as a poet might seek the excitement of inspiration in itself in writing poetry:

> Her deity was impartial; as the radium gathered electric current under her left knee, she knew her high-powered deity was waiting. He would sting her knee and she would hold muscles tense, herself only a sexless wire that was one fire for the fulfillment. She was sexless, being one chord, drawn out, waiting the high-powered rush of the electric fervor. It crept up the left side, she held it, timed it, let it gather momentum, let it gather force; it escaped her above the hip-bone, spread, slightly weakened, up the back-bone; at the nape, it broke, distilled radium into the head but did not burst out of the hair. She wanted the electric power to run on through her, then out, unimpeded by her mind.

The rimes, the repetitions of the incantation, would hold the serpent power mounting in the work, to time it, "let it gather momentum, let it gather force." In shaman rite and yoga rite men have come into heavens or crowns or nirvanas of a thought beyond thought, like the poet inspired, carried away by words until vision arises, as of the whole.

But this blowing one's top or the Taoist ecstatic's churning the milky way with his lion tongue is fearful. The snake in the spinal tree of life has made a nightmare of impending revelation for me, for he wears still the baleful head of the diamondback rattler, the hooded fascination of the king cobra. The Nagas that sway above the Buddha's dreaming form keep my thought away from him.

For a moment this power, this would-be autistic force of the poem, glints forth in *The Walls Do Not Fall:* "or the erect king-cobra crest / to show how the worm turns" and then, where "we" refers to the poet-initiates:

> So we reveal our status
> with twin-horns, disk, erect serpent.

"Walk carefully, speak politely," she warns, for words conceal meanings, "in man's very speech"—as in the world, "insignia"

> in the heron's crest,
> the asp's back,

Is it to hide the serpent power that Helen, evoking Isis, in *Helen in Egypt* would "blacken her face like the prophetic *femme noire* of antiquity"?

> How could I hide my eyes?
>
> how could I veil my face?
> with ash or charcoal from the embers?

Helen thinks, but Achilles already sees something in her and turns upon her in horror:

> What sort of enchantment is this?
> what art will you yield with a fagot?
> are you Hecate? are you a witch?
>
> a vulture? a hieroglyph?

Vulture crown but also serpent crown. The eyes of the woman in Stuck's painting *Die Sünde* watch with the eyes of the anaconda or boa constrictor who is coiled about her, its head flattened in the nape of her seductive neck. Lying in wait. In the depths of intimacy, the hidden will show itself to strike. In such flashes of hate, the Great Mother shows her Hecate face. The jeweled and painted fan upon the floor of the dream was I had to remember the spread hood of a cobra treacherously disguised. "Hated of all Greece!" the cry rings as a refrain in *Helen in Egypt,* an echo or imitation of "Desired of all Greece." And now with naked feet I walked among snakes. In the Hindoo story a wife walking so at night in the dark wood among snakes proves the strength of her faith and devotion to a new Master over Love.

But the Pythian oracles, shamanesses of Attic snake cult, the bird priest-esses in winged and feathered robes of owl or sea-hawk, the carrion Lilith or Eve with her familiar, must have turned fanatical eyes, painted eyes of peacock blue and red and gold, cobra eyes. Angry hurt and hurting eyes. Fearful eyes. The gorgonian mask whose snaky locks writhe with power.

September 3, 1964

"An art is vital only so long as it is interpretive," Pound proposes in *Psychology and the Troubadours:* "so long, that is, as it manifests something which the artist perceives at greater intensity, and more intimately, than his public."

"We have about us the universe of fluid force, and below us the germinal universe of wood alive, of stone alive," he continues: "When we do get into the contemplation of the flowing we find sex, or some correspondence to it, 'positive and negative,' 'North and South,' 'sun and moon.'"

> For the particular parallel I wish to indicate, our handiest illustrations are drawn from physics: 1st, the common electric machine, the glass disc and rotary brushes; 2nd, the wireless telegraph receiver. In the first we generate a current, or if you like, split up a static condition of things and produce a tension. This is focussed on two brass knobs or "poles." These are first in contact, and after the current is generated we can gradually widen the distance between them, and a spark will leap across it, the wider the stronger, until with the ordinary sized laboratory appliance it will leap over or around a large obstacle or pierce a heavy book cover. In the telegraph we have a charged surface— produced in a cognate manner—attracting to it, or registering movements in the invisible aether.

The *trobar clus,* cult of love in Provence that was also a cult of poetry, was "an art, that is to say, a religion," Pound suggests, of a way to the experience of "our kinship with the vital universe." "Did this 'close ring,' this aristocracy of emotion, evolve, out of its half memories of Hellenistic mysteries, a cult—a cult stricter, or more subtle, than that of the celibate ascetics, a cult for the purgation of the soul by the refinement of, and lordship over, the senses?" Does the Lady stand to the lover, as his Muse to the poet, to inspire and cooperate in the art, to demand and command in the name of Amor or of Poetry—a new Master over the Art, so that the poet gives his will, his hunger and the satisfaction of his hunger over to a higher authority— donna della mia mente—that appears to him in the art. In faith he writes in the dark upon a ground that may writhe with the thrill in which he walks, but, devoted to the rule of the art, he is saved in the increase of his phantasy.

In the heightened state, exceeding immediate satisfaction, the goal of genital release is increased from a physical to a spiritual tension, and the original object becomes an instrument towards a sublimation. "The Greek aesthetic would seem to consist wholly in plastic, or in plastic moving towards coitus, and limited by incest, which is the sole Greek taboo," Pound observes in the *Cavalcanti* essay. In the aesthetic of Provence "the conception of the body as a perfect instrument of the increasing intelligence pervades"; beyond the sensory reality, "the impact of light on the eye," and its ideal forms, in the spirit of Romance, the poets sought "an interactive force: the *virtu*." A magic begins, and the poem as an operation of the new theurgy—love, sexual intercourse, as operations of the new theurgy—becomes otherworldly centered. Beatrice and Virgil, spiritual beings, are the true inspirations and hence critics of *The Divine Comedy*. In the high humor of the tradition, Blake will truly declare that he writes not for this world but for his true muses or lovers or readers in the spirit.

"Sex is, that is to say, of a double function and purpose, reproductive and educational; or," Pound continues in *Psychology and the Troubadours:* "as we see in the realm of the fluid force, one sort of vibration produces at different intensities, heat and light." Then:

"The problem, in so far as it concerns Provence, is simply this: Did this 'chivalric love,' this exotic, take on mediumistic properties? Stimulated by the color or quality of emotion, did that 'color' take on forms interpretive of the divine order? Did it lead to an 'exteriorization of the sensibility,' and interpretation of the cosmos by feeling?"

"Thirteen years ago I lost a brother," Blake writes to his patron Hayley, upon the death of Hayley's son in May of 1800: "and with his spirit I converse daily and hourly in the spirit, and see him in my remembrance, in the regions of my imagination. I hear his advice, and even now write from his dictate." And in a letter to Flaxman in September that same year, he writes: "And Now Begins a New life, because another covering of Earth is shaken off. I am more famed in Heaven for my works than I could well conceive. In my Brain are studies & Chambers filled with books & pictures of old, which I wrote & painted in ages of Eternity before my mortal life, & those works are the delight & Study of Archangels. . . . I see our houses of Eternity, which can never be separated, tho' our Mortal vehicles should stand at the remotest corners of heaven from each other."

In his excited state—"my enthusiasm," he calls it in his letter to Hayley, "which I wish all to partake of, since it is to me a source of immortal joy.

... By it I am the companion of Angels"—Blake sees in terms of his Divine World, radiated with Love, a feeling as in Heaven above earthly feeling. This "Above" in Blake contrasts sharply with a "Below"—there seems to be a gap in feeling; for Hayley in Blake's earthy moods is "Pick Thank" and Flaxman, "Sculptor of Eternity," is "Blockhead." Between 1808 and 1811, feeling mocked by Flaxman who had been his teacher and driven by Hayley who all Blake's life was his patron or "angel," Blake reviled them in epigrams and verses:

> Anger & Wrath my bosom rends:
> I thought them the Errors of friends.
> But all my limbs with warmth glow:
> I find them the Errors of the foe.

He had come to suspect that Hayley was patronizing and that Flaxman put him down as a madman. Hayley's commissions for prints that had not been done yet pressed him and then depressed him. "I curse & bless Engravings alternately, because it takes so much time & is so untractable, tho' capable of such beauty & perfection," he writes Hayley or, again: "Your eager expectation of hearing from me compels me to write immediately," Hayley's very "generous & tender solicitude," Blake calls it when Hayley paid his bail and court costs in Blake's sedition trial, leave the artist feeling indebted and driven. "I received your kind letter with the note to Mr. Payne, and have had the cash from him."

"Mr. Flaxman advises that the drawing of Mr. Romney's which shall be chosen instead of the Witch (if that cannot be recovered), be 'Hecate,' the figure with the torch and snake, which he thinks one of the finest drawings."

September 4, 1964

Joey, the "Mechanical Boy," of Bruno Bettelheim's study in the *Scientific American*, March 1959 ("A case history of a schizophrenic child who converted himself into a 'machine' because he did not dare be human"), lives as a creature in a world created by an inaccessible creator, as a machine charged by invisible "pretend" electricity. "He functioned as if by remote control, run by machines of his own powerfully creative fantasy. Not only did he himself believe that he was a machine but, more remarkably, he created this impression in others," Bettelheim tells us. "Entering the dining room, for example, he would string an imaginary wire from his 'energy source'—

an imaginary outlet—to the table. There he 'insulated' himself with paper napkins and finally plugged himself in. . . . So skillful was the pantomime that one had to look twice to be sure there was neither wire nor outlet nor plug. Children and members of our staff spontaneously avoided stepping on the 'wires' for fear of interrupting what seemed the source of his very life."

The higher claim to reality of Joey's created world over the uncreated world is a counterpart of the higher reality the world of his creation has for the artist over the world as material from which it is drawn. The "charge" we feel in the recognition of high art, the breaking through into special truths or keys of existence, is a power the artist has evoked in transforming a content from a private into a communal fantasy. At certain conjunctions, where form and content are suddenly revealed in full, waves of excitement, as if a current had been turned on, pass over the brain and through the nervous systems, and the body seems tuned up in apprehension of what is happening in the work of art. "Many times a day," Bettelheim tells us, Joey "would turn himself on until he 'exploded,' screaming 'Crash, crash!' and hurling items from his ever present apparatus—radio tubes, light bulbs, even motors. . . ." It is as if he were seized by the reality of his conception. It is not Joey's retreat into a private world that we experience, but rather the intensity of his communication, the obliterating power of the language he has made, that takes over not only his reality but also that of those about him. Even at night he is governed by his work, fixing apparatus to his bed to "live him" during his sleep, "contrived from masking tape, cardboard, wire and other paraphernalia." With such an intensity, Orpheus in Harold Dull's poem transforms the actual events of his life into fantastic events— questions that refuse their answers—that are really strings upon a lyre that is a triumph of the imagination. The poet would give himself over to the charge of song, or, beyond poetry, the seer Blake would give himself over to the charge of vision, as Joey gives himself over to the charge of his made-up machine.

Certainly at times we confront in Joey's work the operations of meta- phor, correspondence, persona, and wordplay that govern the poem, and like the poet, Joey must be obedient to laws that appear in the structure he makes. "He was unable to designate by its true name anything to which he attached feelings. Nor could he name his anxieties except through neologisms or word contaminations." But the artist too must find new names and knows that the true name is hidden in the work he must do, as Isis knows that Ra's Secret Name is not the name that all men know but is hidden in his breast. ("They are anagrams, cryptograms, / little boxes, conditioned / to hatch but- terflies," we remember from *The Walls Do Not Fall*.)

"For a long time he spoke about 'master paintings' and 'a master paint-ing room,'" Bettelheim continues, and translates "(i.e. masturbating and masturbating room)." But now it is as if "masturbating" were not the true word until we also understand it is "master painting," an ideogram is form-ing that when complete may reveal the hidden, as yet unexperienced, term; something that masturbating and master painting are but instances of. As here, from Orpheus transforming his life into an instrument of music, or Nathalie Saunderson transforming her sexual seizure into an electricity, or Pound's concept of a universe of fluid force, Joey's idea of being lived by an electric current, I would gather a picture of a power the artist knows in which the fictional real becomes most veridical, in which art comes closest to religion—as in Blake's world, in which man appears as a creature of his own creative force.

Like the poet, Joey must face his adversary in his work. "One of his machines, the 'criticizer,' prevented him from 'saying words which have un-pleasant feelings.' Yet he gave personal names to the tubes and motors in his collection of machinery. Moreover," Bettelheim tells us, "these dead things had feelings; the tubes bled when hurt and sometimes got sick." The excite-ment and the discharge of excitement in the work of art, "master painting," and the aesthetic requirement, the inbuilt 'criticizer' of the artist that deter-mines appropriate material, appear in a grotesque guise in Joey's universe. His tubes and motors are personae of his poem that has overcome all terms of identity outside of its own operation; as in *Good Frend,* Claribel, no more than a name, is so a person. Joey's tubes and motors are not dead things, for they are words in a language that would be living. Deprived of com-munication, for the adults about him would not listen, "When he began to master speech, he talked only to himself." We gather that his parents cut off that current of questioning by which a child participates in first communi-cations, taking apart and putting together the machinery of language which before he had known only as a vehicle of electric emotions and persuasions. But Joey turns to another mute or frozen language embodied in man-made objects about him. "At an early date he became preoccupied with machinery, including an old electric fan which he could take apart and put together again with surprising deftness."

Bettelheim is concerned with the loss of the flow of feeling, represented in the universe of Joey by the need to be turned on or charged; but we are concerned here with how Joey's powerful creative fantasy is like the poet's creative fantasy, the poetic imagination that must have a higher claim to reality than immediate "distractions," in order for the poem to come into being, and how much Joey, run by his own fantastic machinery, is like the inspired poet in his divine madness. Pound, Williams, and H. D. do not make that romantic claim, but all three are disturbed by the power of words over them. Memory (the past), awareness (the immediate), wish (the future) are all heightened and demand satisfaction in the excitement of the work; and more, in that nexus of three, a creativity is at work to change the nature of truth. Blake gave the Imagination highest authority and sought to live in Creation. He could call up the shades of Moses and the Prophets, Homer, Dante, Milton—"majestic shadows, grey but luminous, and superior to the common height of men" and converse with them by the seashore. In his marginalia to Lavater's *Aphorisms* Blake writes: "As we cannot experience pleasure but by means of others who experience either pleasure or pain thro' us, and as all of us on earth are united in thought, for it is impossible to think without images of somewhat on earth. So it is impossible to know God or heavenly things without conjunction with those who know God and heavenly things. Therefore all who converse in the spirit converse with spirits."

> Such tricks hath strong imagination
> That if it would but apprehend some joy
> It comprehends some bringer of that joy.

There is a story that when Blake was making a drawing of "The Ghost of a Flea" the sitter inconsiderately opened his mouth. The artist, "prevented from proceeding with the first sketch," listened to the Flea's conversation and made a separate study of the open mouth.

Joey lives in the Imagination deprived of the current of human friendship except for the love and care invested in the machines about him. He does not retreat to become a 'mechanical boy' ("because he did not dare be human," Bettelheim sees it)—but he advances in the one initiation into human spirit opened to him, the area of achievement and wish embodied in the operations of electrical and plumbing systems, even as in words it is the human work embodied that makes possible the formation of consciousness. The shapes of Homer, Dante, Milton gathered in the mind in the magic of Blake's intense reading, as a person of the electric fan—the human invention—gathered in Joey's mind in the magic of his intense taking apart and putting together again, cast shadows "superior to the common height of men," as Joey was convinced, Bettelheim tells us, that machines were superior to people, or Plato that ideas were superior to things. "If madness and absurdity be synonyms, which they are not, then Blake would be as 'mad as a March hare,'" Samuel Palmer wrote to Mrs. Gilchrist in 1862: "for his love of art was so great that he would see nothing *but art* in anything he loved." So Joey in his love for mechanism saw nothing but mechanism in what he loved. Language may mean all to me, more than art, for the universe seems striving to speak and the burden of life to be to understand what is being said in words that are things and persons and events about us.

"Not every child who possesses a fantasy world is possessed by it," Bettelheim observes: "Normal children may retreat into realms of imaginary glory or magic powers, but they are easily recalled from these excursions. Disturbed children are not always able to make the return trip." And those who know no disturbance of reality, we would add, cannot make the trip out at all.

The shaman's trip to the Other World, the medium's trip to the Astral field, the poet's trip to Hell, Purgatory and Heaven, is a counterpart of the dreamer's trip to the dream or the child's trip to the land he plays. In the process of realization, the Creator must so go into the whole of His Creation in order to create it that it becomes the most real and He becomes most real in it. In the full power of the Imagination, Creation is all, and Who had been Creator is now Creature. God is immanent in the Universe, and incarnate in a person. This is one of the mysteries of the human Christos. Here too there must be a round-trip, the return to God, but it must also be not easy but the least easy of all recallings, for Christ's apotheosis in hubris must be fulfilled in crucifixion. In the full Christian persuasion—most high divine madness—there is a triumph of creativity: the Eternal insists that He has had a lifetime and death in history; the Supreme Fiction insists that It has had a personality in the nonfictional Jesus.

October 1, 1964

To be easily recalled from these excursions, to possess a fantasy world and not to be possessed by it—the way of normal children—is achieved by keeping in mind that the imaginary is not real, that such areas of the psyche's life are no more than child's play, that it is no more than a story. Here, in the fairy tale, taking place in whatever far country and having that time between once upon a time and forever after, stored away for children in the minds of their old nurses and, since the seventeenth century, in a new literary form initiated by the *Contes de ma mère l'oie* of Charles Perrault, the nursery romance, the subversive force of man's creativity hides in an amusement. "In den alten Zeiten, wo das Wünschen noch geholfen hat"—in the old times, when Wishing still could help—the German folk märchen begins, and in the guise of entertainment, the old woman imparts to her infant audience news of the underworld of man's nature, of betrayals and cheats, of ogres and murderers, thieves and shape-changers. They learn to mistrust the real, but they learn also the wishes and powers of old religions and states that have fallen away. The fairy tale is the immortal residue of the spirit that seeks to find its place in the hearts of each generation. As in the twelfth century, religious mysteries and erotic formulations found immortal life in the high romances of the Arthurian cycles, so the folk world perpetuated itself in the yarns spun at the hearthside, and even now, when the spinning wheel has gone from the household way and the fireplace has lost its central function there, the märchen has survived in book form, rescued by the devoted Brothers Grimm. As, again, in the court nurseries of *le Roi Soleil*, like bees secreting the royal jelly to feed the possibility of a queen, imparting style and sentiment, plot and wish, to life, a group of courtiers, after the revocation of the Edict of Nantes, as if apprehending the death of their way—Perrault, then the Countesses de Murat, d'Aulnoy, d'Auneuil, and the Count de Caylus—write their *Cabinets des Fées*. When the dust of the revolutionary tumbrels and the blood of the guillotine have come and gone, and the bourgeoisie, the merchants, industrialists, and managers of our age, have taken over, Perrault's Cinderella, like the Queen of Elfland who carried away Thomas of Erceldoune, would carry away the young from the common sense of a protestant and capitalist reality into her irresponsible romance, the unreal of falling in love and being loved. Early in the process of the Christian era, Augustine, inspired by a most Puritanical demon of righteousness, had warned against such a corporeal light that "seasoneth the life of this world for her blind lovers, with an enticing and dangerous sweetness" and deplored the lot of those who are misled by required love. Yet the ghosts of the dead, of defeated forces in history, survive in the fascination of the living. When the last nobility had died out in the nobility and the rule of public utilities succeeded, Beauty and The Beast from Madame Leprince de Beaumont's eighteenth-century tale, as well as Oedipus from the drama of Sophocles, revive in the art of Cocteau.

March 15, Wednesday. 1961

"Hellenic perfection of style . . ."

In the book *The Hedgehog,* written at Vaud, 1925, the Greek gods belong to the story-world, and, in turn, the little girl Madge, who may be, as H. D.'s daughter Perdita was that year, six, who lives then in an age previous to reading, figures out the actual world with information from stories her mother has told her so that her own experience becomes a story. "The stories weren't just stories," Madge's mother tells her, "but there was something in them like the light in the lamp that isn't the lamp." She sees things in story-light, and in this light Pan, Weltgeist, Our-Father-Which-Art, are lights in turn in the world about her which is a lamp to see by.

Madge in her story is searching for a secret word. It is a matter of the open secret of Goethe, there, everywhere, a word everyone uses, but only experience unlocks the meaning "*Hérisson.*" Don't find the word too quickly; mistake it in order to look for it. The girl Madge knows French, but she does not know what this word *hérisson* is. "Vipers!" Madame Beaupère exclaims, "You should have a hedgehog"—but she is French—"*Hérisson*" she says. Madge "somehow for the moment couldn't remember just what was a *hérisson.*" "'Ah,' said Madge knowingly, 'but yes, the very thing, a hedgehog.' She said hedgehog in French, not knowing what it meant." She must set out in quest of the word in the world.

In *Tribute to the Angels,* twenty years later, we find just such a riddle or search for a name again:

> it lives, it breathes,
> it gives off—fragrance?
>
> I do not know what it gives,
> a vibration that we can not name
>
> for there is no name for it;
> my patron said, "*name it*";
>
> I said, I can not name it,
> there is no name;
>
> he said,
> "invent it."

So in 1912 Pound had given a name "Imagism" to something required in poetry, and returning to the propositions of the 1912 Credo we can see in "Direct treatment of the 'thing'" and in "To use absolutely no word that does not contribute to the presentation" the directive towards an art that strives to find in the image a secret name or password in which "thing" and "word" will become presentation. But this name "Imagism" bound. There was an excitement of introducing the new Imagist poets in *The Egoist* and the excitement too of not knowing what it meant. May Sinclair said that H. D. was *the* Imagist, an epitome. Had she achieved the definitive Imagist poem? But then, Pound had said that he launched the word to define the poetry of H. D. And he had meant too to confine her work to what he had admired.

The idea of H. D.'s cut-stone, pure, terse line was her own version in part, a demand of her temperament that fitted the Credo's demand for a literary functionalism, a clean line against ornament. In her note to the Euripides translations that appear in *The Egoist* in 1915 she writes that she sought "rhymeless hard rhythms" to capture "the sharp edges and irregular cadence of the original." But these hard rhythms, sharp edges and irregular cadences are not only of the original but of a modernist aesthetic in painting, music, and architecture, where ornament, as in poetry rhetoric, was coming to be a term of derogation.

Early poems like "The Contest" with its *"you are chiselled like rocks / that are eaten into by the sea"* or "Sea Lily," where the flower petal is *"with hard edge, / like flint / on a bright stone"* operate to define the meaning of the Imagist poem as well as the quality of the immediate image; as early titles *Hymen* or *Heliodora* contributed to the idea of a new Hellenism. Idea and ideal are as essential to the image as the immediate sensory presentation. To dig the poem we must be receptive, back of these images of free wild elements in nature, and of sheltered gardens, of delicate stony flowers, and of flowers torn and trampled under foot, of unruly surfs, not only to presences of gods and daemons, the elementary idols of the poem, but to the temper of the verse itself, the ideal of human spirit presented. "Posing," the unkind were likely to judge it, but for her kind H. D.'s tone presented a key in which to live. This ideal is what in my generation Charles Olson has called a stance. Poetic will is involved, awkwardly at first, trying, in what we call style or tone, but it would go beyond manner, to take over and make its own definition of poetry, where we strive to exemplify something we desire in our nature. "There was about her," Williams writes of H. D. in his *Autobiography:* "that which is found in wild animals at times, a breathless impatience, almost a silly unwillingness to come to the point." But now, seeing past Williams's meaning to convince us that he was not taken in by H. D. and even, we are aware, to stir up our disaffections—seeing, past that, the content here with the role in mind that idea and ideal have in the artist's search for a definition of what he is to be, Williams does give us telling details. "She said that when she wrote it was a great help, she'd splash ink on her clothes to give her a feeling of freedom and indifference toward the mere means of the writing."

If in Imagist poems like "Heat" there had been as well as the perfectionism, the intense realization of an instant in time, the prayer for life beyond perfection and realization, in *The Hedgehog,* having "almost a silly unwillingness to come to the point," the mode of story exorcizing the mode of image, there is a first statement as early as 1925 of the sense of life as an intellectual and spiritual adventure that is to become the dominant mode of H. D.'s imagination in the major phase that begins with *The War Trilogy.* We have taken *Ion* as a turning point, with its commentary that incorporates poetic experience and psychoanalytic experience to give depth and complexity of meaning to form and content: now, not only an intensity of image, not only a style, but also a perception in organization, a way, is to be essential in the creative force of her work. We may take *The Hedgehog* as an announcement. It seems isolated, her only children's book; the Greek world in story is so different from the Greek world in the "intellectual and emotional complex in an instant of time" that the Imagist Credo demanded. And it is different too from the exalted, enthralled or ecstatic voice of the personae of H. D., whether of the poems of the Lawrencian period—"Adonis," "Pygmalion," or "Eurydice"—or of the Sapphic fragments, or of the prose of *Palimpsest;* for a new voice, the common sense of the wise nurse telling what life is like to the child, or the questing sense of the child seeking in a story to find out what is going on, enters in. H. D. will all her life be concerned in her work with conveying to our sympathy the fact that agony seems to be in the very nature of deep experience, that in every instant there is a painful—painful in its intensity—revelation. In *Palimpsest,* Hipparchia, Raymonde, and Helen Fairwood agonize; the interior monologue means to communicate the impact of ineffable experience. But in *The Hedgehog,* Madge's interior monologue is talking to herself in search of a language. The meaning of *hérisson* is not beyond finding out, but it is postponed until Madge can gather, asking from everyone and from everything, the most common sense— the communality—of what it is. In the very opening of the book, the lead is given. *Quoi donc?* And then: "Which means," Madge recognizes: "well what do you mean by trying to tell me that anything like that means what you seem to think it means." The adventure is the old guessing game *I am thinking of a word; What is it?* and Madge seeks to find out a definition that does not confine.

She seeks too to find a definition of her self that does not confine, as H. D. was seeking to do in her own life. And Madge trying out her style can miss. In talking with Madame Beaupère, she speaks "in such a funny unnatural affected little way" at one point that Madame Beaupère is put off, and Madge perceives "that her grown-up manner had not quite worked." But the ideal is rightly a matter of trial for it is part of the searching out of means towards feeling: "she thought and practiced it, in order to give her a feeling of freedom and indifference," as later, H. D.'s ideal of the Hellenic tries to reach the feeling of hardness and perfection. And does, for what changes in H. D.'s concept is not that the feeling of hardness and perfection ceases to be desired but that other feelings enter in to the picture. "Echo is easy to find," Madge knows, "and the boy Narcissus," but "Some of the light-in-lamp people you look for and never find."

In Homer we know it is all a story told, as Shakespeare would remind us, even while we are entranced, that this "life" is a stage upon which actors play. This is their nurse voice, when even the greatest poets amuse us as if they were giant maids and we were children. So Cocteau and Bergman would involve us beyond the being moved in the moving pictures in the knowledge throughout that we entertain their entertainment. It is in the mystery of the Muses that we transcend belief and disbelief and follow the story, for the story-teller has as part of his art not only that he leads us into the magic realms but that he can recall us from the excursion. Where there is no story magic, blood will be blood and pain pain so that misled, carried away, the child is hurt and cries out or is afraid. In Flaherty's film of Samoan life, I fainted during the tatooing ritual, flooded with the apprehension of pain. But in story, in the self-mutilation of Oedipus or the immolation of Christ the pain is not a thing in itself but belongs to a configuration of action, fulfills and leads on. My mother would lean over in the dark of the movie house to recall me: "it is only a movie, it is just a movie," she would whisper. Shakespeare's actors reminding us that it is but a stage seem finally to be saying that our actual life is only a stage from which we may be recalled at death. And Christ in the testimony of St. John at Ephesus told his beloved disciple that the death upon the cross was but a figure in a dance—"and if you have not entered the dance, you mistake the event." "Growing up and last year's shoes that didn't fit this year—these were things that were part of a dream, not part of reality," Madge thinks: "Reality was the Erlking and moonlight on Bett's room wall."

The story-telling voice of The Hedgehog enters into the commentary of Ion in whose voice the Greek drama appears in the guise of fairy tale. And the address of the opening of The Walls Do Not Fall establishes such a voice in which we are aware of the story-teller and his following, the I and a you in which the individual reader is but one; "from your (and my) old town square," belongs to the nurse's art, drawing us into the realm of her telling. The "we" and the "they" are people of the story, as the "I" is at one time a person of the story—"I sense my own limit" is part of what she has to tell—and the poet who may address her audience as well as the "they" of the poem: "but if you do not even understand what words say, / how can you expect to pass judgment / on what words conceal?" Those of the audience who are with her will think of themselves as "we," those who are not in it and would interrupt will think of themselves as "they." And the story-teller anticipates their doubts of the story and exhorts them to surrender: "*Let us substitute / enchantment for sentiment.*" Yes, she continues: "*re-dedicate our gifts / to spiritual realism*"; but it is all to be "*a Tale told of a Jar or jars,*" having the truth of what "*we are told.*" In *Helen in Egypt,* which H. D. saw as her culminating master work, Helen is entirely a creature of story, having her life in all that has been told of her.

There remains the actual feeling, a Greece that is all H. D.'s. She evokes a realm of pagan things—hinterlands of the psyche—but also inner qualities of places and times, woodlands, sea-coasts, gardens, mountain ledges. In *Hedylus* the stranger-father-critic says to the young poet: "Your idea of the rock-ridge becoming re-divided into separate efflorescence, according to the altitude, implying, as I judge, a spiritual comparison as well as a mere natural one, is unique, differing in all particulars from anything I have yet met with."

It was not pure beauty, or it was something besides pure beauty, that even the poems that gave rise to H. D.'s repute for the rare and pure strove to capture, but beauty or perfection as it was a key somewhere to the nature of event, and finally, as it played its part in the development of the story.

Yes, but this striving was not only to capture a quality in what she had known, but was to challenge experience itself in turn to yield a quality. "Beauty" was from the first, as in the review of Marianne Moore's work or in the poem "The Tribute" she makes clear, a battle-cry, a cause. The Image too was a demand as well as a response.

In December 1916, reviewing Fletcher's *Goblins and Pagodas* in *The Egoist,* she criticizes or challenges "certain current opinions concerning the so-called *new poetry,*" and against the proposition of the images upon a Greek vase as things of art, self-contained images, she proposes: "How much more than the direct image to him are the images suggested by shadow and light, the flicker of the purple wine, the glint across the yellow, the depth of the crimson and red. . . . When the wine itself within the great jar stands waiting for him." Then: "He uses the direct image, it is true, but he seems to use it as a means of evoking other and vaguer images—a pebble, as it were, dropped into a quiet pool, in order to start across the silent water, wave on wave of light, of color, of sound."

There is at least the possibility that whatever battle-cry of "Beauty" or idea of the fine-wrought image, there was also another thing a poem was— "a pebble . . . dropped into a quiet pool" to set up reverberations in life so that "Here," "there," Greece and its things, old gods and pagan places or the mode of story, enlived consciousness in living, made it moving with

"wave on wave of light, of color, of sound." Story, like perspective in painting, may be an invention to satisfy a need in experience for design, to build
a house for feeling in time or space. Does story stand within the actual life
or the actual life experience stand within the story as the wine itself is stored
in the great jar upon whose surfaces the artist has painted his image of the
wine and the jar?

The threads interweaving create a close intricate field of feeling; and we
admire the work in which there is no ornament dismissed but where light
flows from what we took to be ornament and proves to be essential. In the
shuttle flying under the swift sense of the work, the "incident here and there"
gathers so many instances from themselves into a moving significance, un-
folding or discovering a design, that we see now the art was to set things
into movement, was not only the weaving of a work of art but as if each
knot that bound the whole into the quiet of a unity were also the pebble
that dropped into that quiet as a pool broke up, was knot but also slipping-
of-the-knot, to set up an activity throughout in the work of time and space
within time and space.

The sense that "*we are at the cross-roads*" then has structural as well
as historical and psychological meaning in *The War Trilogy*. Given the name
Imagiste, H. D. was never satisfied that it meant what she seemed to think
it meant, and even after her analysis with Freud, she did not rest with the
Freudian image but went on to the *eidola* of *Helen in Egypt*. What was
required was that there be the full power of a double meaning, that the real
refuse to be defined. In word and image and then in story her sense was
always that "the tide is turning."

Chronology

1886   Hilda Doolittle is born September 10 in Bethlehem, Pennsylvania, to Helen Wolle Doolittle and Professor Charles Leander Doolittle.

1895   Father leaves Lehigh University to join the faculty of the University of Pennsylvania; the family moves to Philadelphia.

1896   Professor Doolittle is appointed Flower Professor of Astronomy and Founding Director of the Flower Observatory at the University of Pennsylvania.

1901   H. D. makes the acquaintance of Ezra Pound.

1904   Enters Bryn Mawr College. One of her classmates is the poet Marianne Moore.

1906   H. D. withdraws from college because of poor health. For the next five years she lives and studies at home. She begins to work seriously at writing.

1911   H. D. travels to Europe, decides to reside in England, and through Pound meets Richard Aldington, F. S. Flint, Brigit Patmore, T. E. Hulme, and other literary figures.

1913   Marries the poet, Richard Aldington. The first poems by "H. D., Imagiste" are published in *Poetry* magazine.

1916   H. D. takes over as assistant editor of *The Egoist,* replacing her husband who enters the army. H. D. holds this position until 1917 when she is succeeded by T. S. Eliot. She publishes *Sea Garden* and *Choruses from the Iphigenia in Aulis,* a translation.

1918   Brother is killed in action in France. She meets Bryher (Winifred Ellerman) who becomes her lover and benefactor.

1919   H. D. gives birth to her daughter Perdita. She and Aldington are separated. Her father dies. Another translation, *Choruses from the Iphigenia in Aulis and the Hippolytus* is published.

1920   With Bryher, H. D. travels to Greece in the spring and to America in the fall.

1921   Publishes *Hymen,* a volume of poems.

1922   Travels in America and Greece again with Bryher.

1923   Travels to Egypt with her mother, Perdita, and Bryher.

1924   Publishes *Heliodora and Other Poems.*

1925   The *Collected Poems of H. D.* and a selection from *Hedylus* are published.

1926   *Palimpsest,* a novel.

1927   *Hippolytus Temporizes,* a verse drama. H. D's mother dies.

1928   *Hedylus,* a novel.

1931   *Red Roses for Bronze,* a volume of poems.

1933–34 H. D. undergoes analysis with Freud.

1936   H. D. publishes *The Hedgehog,* a tale for children.

1937   Publishes her translation and commentary, *Euripides' Ion.*

1938   H. D. receives the annual Helen Haire Levinson Prize of *Poetry* magazine. She and Aldington are divorced.

1944   *The Walls Do Not Fall,* the first of the trilogy of war poems.

1945   *Tribute to the Angels,* the second of the trilogy.

1946   *The Flowering of the Rod,* the third of the trilogy.

1949   "By Avon River" is published.

1956   *Tribute to Freud,* an account of her psychoanalysis with Freud.

1957   *Selected Poems of H. D.*

1959   H. D. is awarded the Brandeis University Creative Arts Award
        for Poetry.

1960   H. D. is the first woman to receive the Award of Merit Medal
        for Poetry of the American Academy of Arts and Letters. Her
        novel, *Bid Me to Live (A Madrigal)*, is published.

1961   *Helen in Egypt*, a poem. H. D. dies September 28 in Zurich,
        Switzerland.

1972   *Hermetic Definition*, her last poem, is published posthu-
        mously.

Contributors

HAROLD BLOOM, Sterling Professor of the Humanities at Yale University, is the author of *The Anxiety of Influence, Poetry and Repression,* and many other volumes of literary criticism. His forthcoming study, *Freud: Transference and Authority,* attempts a full-scale reading of all of Freud's major writings. A MacArthur Prize Fellow, he is general editor of five series of literary criticism published by Chelsea House. During 1987–88, he served as Charles Eliot Norton Professor of Poetry at Harvard University.

DENISE LEVERTOV's collections of poetry include *Relearning the Alphabet, The Freeing of the Dust,* and *Candles in Babylon.* Her essays appear in *The Poet in the World.*

NORMAN N. HOLLAND is Professor of English at the University of Florida, Gainesville, and author of *The First Modern Comedies: The Significance of Etheredge, Wycherly, and Congreve, Psychoanalysis and Shakespeare,* and *The Dynamics of Literary Response.*

A. KINGSLEY WEATHERHEAD is Professor of English at the University of Oregon. His works of criticism include *A Reading of Henry Green, The Edge of the Image: Marianne Moore, William Carlos Williams, and Some Other Poets,* and articles on Eliot, Auden, and Durrell.

SUSAN FRIEDMAN is Professor of English at the University of Wisconsin, Madison. She is the author of *Psyche Reborn: The Emergence of H. D.*

SUSAN GUBAR is Professor of English at Indiana University at Bloomington. With Sandra Gilbert, she has written *The Madwoman in the Attic: A Study of Women and the Literary Imagination in the Nineteenth Century.*

LOUIS L. MARTZ, Sterling Professor Emeritus of English at Yale University, is the author of *The Poetry of Meditation, John Donne and Meditation, The*

Paradise Within: Studies in Vaughan, Traherne, and Milton's Poem of the Mind.

ADALAIDE MORRIS teaches English at the University of Iowa. She is the author of *Wallace Stevens: Imagination and Faith.*

ALBERT GELPI is Coe Professor of American Literature at Stanford University. His publications include *Emily Dickinson: The Mind of the Poet, The Poet in America: 1650 to the Present,* and *The Tenth Muse: The Psyche of the American Poet.*

ROBERT DUNCAN's major collections of poetry are *The Opening of the Field, Roots and Branches, Bending the Bow* and *Ground Work.* Associated with both the San Francisco Renaissance and the Black Mountain "school" of poetry, his critical works include *The Truth and Life of Myth* and *The H. D. Book.*

Bibliography

Arthur, Marilyn. "Psychomythology: The Case of H. D." *Bucknell Review* 28, no. 2 (1983): 65–79.

Beck, Joyce Lorraine. "Dead Awakening: A Reading of H. D.'s *Trilogy*." *San Jose Studies* 8, no. 2 (Spring 1982): 59–70.

Bernikow, Louise. "Lovers: Paris in the Twenties." In *Among Women*, 155–92. New York: Harmony Books, 1980.

Bush, Douglas. *Mythology and the Romantic Tradition in English Poetry*, 497–506. Cambridge, Mass.: Harvard University Press, 1937.

Carruth, Hayden. "Poetry Chronicle." *Hudson Review* 27 (1974): 308–20.

Collecott, Diana. Introduction to *The Gift*, by H. D. London: Virago Press, 1984.

Dembo, L. S. "Imagism and Aesthetic Mysticism." In *Conceptions of Reality in Modern American Poetry*, 10–47. Berkeley: University of California Press, 1966.

———. "Norman Holmes Pearson on H. D.: An Interview." *Contemporary Literature* 10 (1969): 435–36.

Diepeveen, Leonard. "H. D. and the Film Arts." *Journal of Aesthetic Education* 18, no. 4 (Winter 1984): 57–65.

Doyle, Charles. "Palimpsests of the Word: The Poetry of H. D." *Queen's Quarterly* 92 (1985): 310–21.

Duncan, Robert. "Beginnings: Chapter 1 of *The H. D. Book*, Part I." *Coyote's Journal* 5–6 (1966): 8–31.

———. "*The H. D. Book*, Part I: Chapter 2." *Coyote's Journal* 8 (1967): 27–35.

———. "Two Chapters from H. D." *Tri-Quarterly* 12 (1968): 67–98.

———. "From *The H. D. Book*, Part I: Beginnings, Chapter 5: Occult Matters." *Stony Brook* 1–2 (Fall 1968): 4–19.

———. "*The H. D. Book*, Part II: Nights and Days, Chapter 4." *Caterpillar* 2, no. 2 (April 1969): 27–60.

———. "From *The H. D. Book*, Part II: Chapter 5 (section one)." *Stony Brook* 3–4 (Fall 1969): 336–47.

———. "Part II, Chapter 5 (section 2)." *Credences* 1, no. 1 (1975): 50–94.

———. "*The H. D. Book*, Part II: Nights and Days, Chapter 9." *Chicago Review* 30, no. 3 (Winter 1979): 37–88.

———. "From *The H. D. Book*, Part 2: Nights and Days, Chapter 11." *Montemora* 8 (1981): 79–113.

DuPlessis, Rachel Blau. "Family, Sexes, Psyche: An Essay on H. D. and the Muse of the Woman Writer." *Montemora* 6 (1979): 137–56.

———. "Romantic Thralldom in H. D." *Contemporary Literature* 26 (1979): 178–203.

———, and Susan Stanford Friedman. "'Woman is Perfect': H. D.'s Debate with Freud." *Feminist Studies* 7 (1981): 417–30.

———. "A Note on the State of H. D.'s *The Gift.*" *Sulfur* 9 (1984): 178–82.

———. *H. D.: The Career of That Struggle.* Brighton: Harvester Press; Bloomington: Indiana University Press, 1986.

Eder, Doris. "Freud and H. D." *Book Forum* 1 (1975): 365–69.

Engel, Bernard F. "H. D.: Poems That Matter and Dilutations." *Contemporary Literature* 10 (1969): 507–22.

Fields, Kenneth. Introduction to *Tribute to Freud,* by H. D. Boston: David R. Godine, 1974.

Firchow, Peter. "Hilda Doolittle 1886–1961." In *American Writers: A Collection of Literary Biographies,* Supplement I, Part I, edited by Leonard Unger, 253–75. New York: Scribner's, 1979.

———. "Rico and Julia: The Hilda Doolittle–D. H. Lawrence Affair Reconsidered." *Journal of Modern Literature* 8 (1980): 51–76.

Freeman, Lucy, and Herbert S. Strean. "The Poet Patient." In *Freud and Women,* 117–22. New York: Ungar, 1981.

Freibert, Lucy. "Conflict and Creativity in the World of H. D." *Women's Studies* 1 (1979): 258–71.

———. "From Semblance to Selfhood: The Evolution of Woman in H. D.'s Neo-Epic *Helen in Egypt.*" *Arizona Quarterly* 36 (1980): 165–75.

Friedberg, Anne. "Approaching *Borderline.*" *Millennium Film Journal* 7–9 (Fall–Winter 1980–81): 130–39.

———. "On H. D.: Woman, History, Recognition." *Wide Angle: A Film Quarterly of Theory, Criticism, and Practice* 5, no. 2 (1982): 26–31.

Friedman, Susan Stanford. "Creating A Woman's Mythology: H. D.'s *Helen in Egypt.*" *Women's Studies* 5 (1977): 163–97.

———. "Psyche Reborn: Tradition, Re-Vision, and the Goddess as Mother-Symbol in H. D.'s Epic Poetry." *Women's Studies* 6 (1979): 147–60.

———, and Rachel Blau DuPlessis. "'I Had Two Loves Separate': The Sexualities of H. D.'s 'Her.'" *Montemora* 8 (1981): 7–30.

———. *Psyche Reborn: The Emergence of H. D.* Bloomington: Indiana University Press, 1981.

———. "'I go where I love': An Intertextual Study of H. D. and Adrienne Rich." *Signs* 9 (1983): 228–45.

———. "'Remembering Shakespeare Always, But Remembering Him Differently': H. D.'s 'By Avon River.'" *Sagetrieb* 2, no. 2 (Summer–Fall 1983): 45–70.

———. "Palimpsest of Origins in H. D.'s Career." *Poesis* 6, nos. 3–4 (Winter 1985): 56–73.

Gage, John T. *In the Arresting Eye.* Baton Rouge: Louisiana State University Press, 1981.

Gelpi, Albert. "The Thistle and the Serpent." In *Notes on Thought and Vision and The Wise Sappho,* by H. D., 7–14. San Francisco: City Lights Books, 1982.

Gibbons, Kathryn Gibbs. "The Art of H. D." *Mississippi Quarterly* 15 (1962): 152–60.

Gould, Jean. "H. D." In *American Women Poets: Pioneers of Modern Poetry,* 151–75. New York: Dodd, Mead, 1980.

Grahn, Judy. *The Highest Apple.* San Francisco: Spinsters Ink, 1985.

Greenwood, E. B. "H. D. and the Problem of Escapism." *Essays in Criticism* 21 (1971): 365–77.

Gregory, Horace. Introduction to *Helen in Egypt,* by H. D. New York: New Directions, 1961.

Gubar, Susan. "Sapphistries." *Signs* 10 (1984): 43–62.

Guest, Barbara. *Herself Defined: The Poet H. D. and Her World.* Garden City, N.Y.: Doubleday, 1984.

———. "The Intimacy of Biography." *Poesis* 6, nos. 3–4 (Winter 1985): 74–83.

Harmer, J. B. *Victory in Limbo: Imagism, 1908–1917.* London: Secker & Warburg, 1975.

Holland, Norman N. *Poems in Persons: An Introduction to the Psychoanalysis of Literature.* New York: Norton, 1973.

Hubbell, Lindley W. "The Last Book of H. D.'s Poetry." *Eigo Seinen* 119 (1973): 286–87.

Hughes, Gertrude. "Arms and the Woman: H. D.'s Revisionary Epic." In *Genius and Gender: Revisionary Visions of Emily Dickinson, H. D., Elizabeth Bishop, Gwendolyn Brooks, and Adrienne Rich.* Middletown, Conn.: Wesleyan University Press, 1985.

Hughes, Glenn. "H. D.: The Perfect Imagist." *Imagism and the Imagists,* 109–24. Stanford: Stanford University Press, 1931.

Jackson, Brendan. " 'The Fulsomeness of Her Prolixity': Reflections on 'H. D., Imagiste' " *South Atlantic Quarterly* 83 (1984): 91–102.

King, Michael. Foreword to *End to Torment: A Memoir of Ezra Pound,* by H. D. Edited by Michael King and Norman Holmes Pearson. New York: New Directions, 1979.

———. Review of *HERmione. Paideuma* 11 (1982): 339–44.

Kloepfer, Deborah Kelly. "Flesh Made Word: Maternal Inscription in H. D." *Sagetrieb* 3 (1984): 27–48.

Knapp, Peggy A. "Women's Freud(e): H. D.'s *Tribute to Freud* and Gladys Schmitt's *Sonnets for an Analyst.*" *Massachusetts Review* 24 (1983): 338–52.

Kunitz, Stanley J. "H. D.'s War Trilogy." In *A Kind of Order, A Kind of Folly: Essays and Conversations,* 204–9. Boston: Little, Brown, 1975.

Lynch, Beverly. "Love, Beyond Men and Women: H. D." In *Lesbian Lives: Biographies of Women from* The Ladder, edited by Barbara Groer and Coletta Reid, 259–72. Oakland: Diana Press, 1976.

Mandel, Charlotte. "Garbo/Helen: The Self-Projection of Beauty by H. D." *Women's Studies* 7 (1980): 127–35.

———. "The Redirected Image: Cinematic Dynamics in the Style of H. D. (Hilda Doolittle)." *Literature/Film Quarterly* 11 (1983): 36–45.

Materer, Timothy. "H. D., Serenitas, and Canto CXIII." *Paideuma* 12 (1983): 275–80.

McAlmon, Robert. "Forewarned as Regards H. D.'s Prose." In *Palimpsest,* by H. D., 241–44. Carbondale: Southern Illinois University Press, 1968.

McNeil, Helen. Introduction to *Her,* by H. D. London: Virago Press, 1984.

Moore, Harry T. Preface to *Palimpsest,* by H. D. Carbondale: Southern Illinois University Press, 1968.

Morley, Hilda. Review of *Collected Poems 1912–1944,* by H. D. *Ironwood* 13 (1985): 159–75.

Morris, Adalaide. "Reading H. D.'s 'Helios and Athene.'" *Iowa Review* 12 (1981): 155–63.

Newlin, Margaret. "'Unhelpful *Hymen*': Marianne Moore and Hilda Doolittle." *Essays in Criticism* 27 (1977): 216–30.

Ostriker, Alicia. "The Thieves of Language: Women Poets and Revisionist Mythmaking." *Signs* 8 (1982): 68–90.

———. "The Poet as Heroine: Learning to Read H. D." *American Poetry Review* 12, no. 2 (1983): 29–38.

———. "What Do Women (Poets) Want: H. D. and Marianne Moore as Poetic Ancestresses." *Poesis* 6, nos. 3–4 (Winter 1985): 1–9.

Pearson, Norman Holmes. Foreword to *Hermetic Definition,* by H. D. New York: New Directions, 1972.

———. Foreword to *Tribute to Freud,* by H. D. New York: New Directions, 1974.

Peck, John. "Passo Perpetuae H. D." *Parnassus: Poetry in Review* 3 (1975): 42–74.

Pondrom, Cyrena N. "Selected Letters from H. D. to F. S. Flint: A Commentary on the Imagist Period." *Contemporary Literature* 10 (1969): 557–86.

———. "H. D. and the Origins of Imagism." *Sagetrieb* 4 (1985): 73–97.

Pratt, William. Review of *HERmione,* by H. D. *World Literature Today* 56 (1982): 690–91.

Quinn, Vincent. *Hilda Doolittle (H. D.).* New York: Twayne, 1967.

———. "H. D.'s *Hermetic Definition*: The Poet as Archetypal Mother." *Contemporary Literature* 18 (1977): 51–61.

Rasula, Jed. "A Renaissance of Women Writers." *Sulfur* 7 (1983): 160–72.

Reeve, F. D. "H. D. Rediviva." *Poetry* 124 (June 1974): 162–67.

Revell, Peter. "'The Meaning That Words Hide . . .'" In *Quest in Modern American Poetry,* 171–98. London: Vision; Totowa, N.J.: Barnes & Noble, 1981.

Riddel, Joseph N. "H. D. and the Poetics of 'Spiritual Realism.'" *Contemporary Literature* 10 (1969): 447–73.

———. "H. D.'s Scene of Writing—Poetry as (and) Analysis." *Studies in the Literary Imagination* 12 (1979): 41–59.

Robinson, Janice S. *H. D.: The Life and Work of an American Poet.* Boston: Houghton Mifflin, 1982.

Romig, Evelyn M. "An Achievement of H. D. and Theodore Roethke: Psychoanalysis and the Poetics of Teaching." *Literature and Psychology* 28, nos. 3–4 (1978): 105–11.

Satterthwaite, Alfred. "John Cournos and H. D." *Twentieth Century Literature* 22 (1976): 394–410.

Scalapino, Leslie. "Re-living." *Poetics* 4 (May 1984): 53–55.

Schaffner, Perdita. "Merano, 1962." *Paideuma* 4 (1975): 513–18.

———. "The Egyptian Cat." In *Hedylus,* by H. D., 142–46. Redding Ridge, Conn.: Black Swan Books, 1980.

———. "Pandora's Box." In *HERmione,* by H. D., vii–xi. New York: New Directions, 1981.

———. "Unless a Bomb Falls . . ." In *The Gift,* by H. D., ix–xv. New York: New Directions, 1982.

———. "A Profound Animal." In *Bid Me to Live (A Madrigal),* by H. D., 185–94. Redding Ridge, Conn.: Black Swan Books, 1983.

Scobey, Katherine. "The Making of a Poet." *The New Journal* 16, no. 4 (February 1984): 27–34.

Scupham, Peter. "H. D." *Agenda* 12, no. 3 (Autumn 1974): 40–44.

Sievert, Heather Rosario. "H. D.: A Symbolist Perspective." *Comparative Literature Studies* 16 (1979): 48–57.

Sisson, C. H. "H. D." *Poetry Nation* 4 (1975): 85–91.

Smith, Paul. "Wounded Woman: H. D.'s Post-Imagist Writing." In *Pound Revised,* 110–32. London: Croom Helm, 1983.

Swann, Thomas Burnett. *The Classical World of H. D.* Lincoln: University of Nebraska Press, 1962.

Thurley, Geoffrey. "Phenomenalist Idioms: Doolittle, Moore, Levertov." In *The American Moment: American Poetry in the Mid-Century,* 109–25. London: Edward Arnold, 1977.

Wagner, Linda Welshimer. "*Helen in Egypt:* A Culmination." *Contemporary Literature* 10 (1969): 523–36.

Wallace, Emily. "Afterword: The House of the Father's Science and the Mother's Art." *William Carlos Williams Newsletter* 2, no. 2 (1976): 4–5.

———. "Athene's Owl." *Poesis* 6, nos. 3–4 (Winter 1985): 98–123.

Watts, Harold H. "H. D. and the Age of Myth." *Sewanee Review* 56 (1948): 287–303.

White, Eric W. *Images of H. D.* London: Enitharmon Press, 1976.

Wolle, Francis. "Hilda Doolittle: The Poet H. D." In *A Moravian Heritage,* 55–60. Boulder: Empire Reproduction and Printing, 1972.

Acknowledgments

"H. D.: An Appreciation" by Denise Levertov from *Poetry* 100, no. 3 (June 1962) by Denise Levertov, © 1962 by Denise Levertov Goodman. Reprinted by permission. This essay later appeared in *The Poet in the World,* © 1962 by Denise Levertov Goodman. Reprinted by permission of the author and New Directions Publishing Co.

"*Tribute to Freud* and the H. D. Myth" (originally entitled "H. D. and the Blameless Physician") by Norman N. Holland from *Contemporary Literature* 10, no. 4 (Autumn 1969), © 1969 by the Board of Regents of the University of Wisconsin System. Reprinted by permission of the University of Wisconsin Press.

"Style in H. D.'s Novels" by A. Kingsley Weatherhead from *Contemporary Literature* 10, no. 4 (Autumn 1969), © 1969 by the Board of Regents of the University of Wisconsin System. Reprinted by permission of the University of Wisconsin Press.

"Who Buried H. D.? A Poet, Her Critics, and Her Place in 'The Literary Tradition'" by Susan Friedman from *College English* 36, no. 7 (March 1975), © 1975 by the National Council of Teachers of English. Reprinted by permission of the publisher and the author.

"The Echoing Spell of H. D.'s *Trilogy*" by Susan Gubar from *Contemporary Literature* 19, no. 2 (Spring 1978), © 1978 by the Board of Regents of the University of Wisconsin System. Reprinted by permission of the University of Wisconsin Press.

"Introduction to *The Collected Poems*" by Louis L. Martz from *H. D.: Collected Poems 1912–1944,* edited by Louis L. Martz, © 1983 by Louis L. Martz. Reprinted by permission of New Directions Publishing Corporation and Carcanet Press Ltd.

"The Concept of Projection: H. D.'s Visionary Powers" by Adalaide Morris from *Contemporary Literature* 25, no. 4 (Winter 1984), © 1984 by the Board of Regents of the University of Wisconsin System. Reprinted by permission of the University of Wisconsin Press.

"H. D.: Hilda in Egypt" by Albert Gelpi from *Coming to Light: American Women Poets in the Twentieth-Century,* edited by Diane Wood Middlebrook and Marilyn Yalom, © 1985 by Albert Gelpi. Reprinted by permission of the author and the University of Michigan Press.

"H. D. Book: Book 2, Chapter 6" by Robert Duncan from *The Southern Review* 21, no. 1 (January 1985), © 1985 by Robert Duncan. Reprinted by permission of the Estate of Robert Duncan.

Index

Achilles (*Helen in Egypt*), 127–28, 131–32, 133–34, 137, 146; biographical basis for, 126–27, 138
Ahlers, Anny, 92
Aldington, Richard, 79, 86, 88, 123, 137; fictional portrayals of, 87, 126–27, 138; infidelities of, 28, 82
"Analysis Terminable and Interminable" (Freud), 16
Antipater of Sidon, 31
Aphrodite (*Helen in Egypt*), 127
Ashton, Julia (*Bid Me to Live*), 29, 38, 39, 40–41
Ashton, Rafe (*Bid Me to Live*), 39, 40, 41, 87
Astrid (*Borderline*), 79, 112–13
Augustine, St., 154
Autobiography (Williams), 81–82, 156

Bachelard, Gaston, 67
Bart, Ray (*Palimpsest*). *See* Ransome, Raymonde
Beauvoir, Simone de, 70
Bella Carter (*Bid Me to Live*). *See* Carter, Bella
Bergman, Ingmar, 158
Bettelheim, Bruno, 149–51, 152, 153
Bid Me to Live (A Madrigal), 10, 39–44, 45, 79; as autobiography, 29, 40, 86–87, 88; cold imagery in, 42; deserted woman in, 82–83; dimensions in, 40–41, 42–43; geometric patterns in, 39, 41–42; passivity in, 34; past as static in, 38; repetition in, 40; source of poetry in, 44; style in, 33, 40

Blake, William, 148–49, 151, 152
Blasting and Bombardiering (Lewis), 29
Blum, Dr. (*The Hedgehog*), 64
Brett, Dorothy, 40
Bridge, The (Crane), 48
Bryher, 86, 87, 114, 115; and Corfu vision, 20, 101, 102; Freudian analysis of, 113; as healer, 30, 36, 89; static imagery of, 38–39
Bush, Douglas, 27, 53

Cantos (Pound), 123, 135
Captain January, 14, 18
Carter, Bella (*Bid Me to Live*), 39–40, 41, 43
Cavalcanti (Pound), 148
Chadwick, Mary, 112
Chicago, Judy, 70
Claribel (*Good Friend*), 142–43, 151
Close Up, 110, 111, 112, 113
Clytemnestra (*Helen in Egypt*), 130
Cocteau, Jean, 154, 158
Collins, H. P., 27
Corfu vision, 16, 65, 114; Freud's interpretation of, 18, 20, 22–23, 24, 116; and H. D.'s writing, 101–2, 103; tripod image in, 19, 21, 65
Cournos, John, 125, 137
Crane, Hart, 48, 75

Da Vinci, Leonardo, 107
Dembo, L. S., 48
Demion (*Hedylus*), 36
Dickinson, Emily, 1, 64, 70, 138–39
"Directive" (Frost), 135
Divine Comedy, The (Dante), 148

176INDEX

"H. D. and the Poetics of 'Spiritual Realism'" (Riddel), 49–50, 51

H. D., works of: "Adonis," 157; "Advent," 88; "Amaranth," 82, 83–84, 89, 91; "Autobiographical Notes," 85; "Body and Soul," 93; *Borderline*, 45, 79, 112–14; "Christmas 1944," 93; "The Cinema and the Classics," 110–11; and cinematography, 110–14; *The Collected Poems 1912–1944*, 1; *Collected Poems (1925)*, 9, 123; "Compassionate Friendship," 125; "The Contest," 156; "The Dancer," 1, 3–4, 92; "Demeter," 28; *End to Torment*, 46, 126; "Envy," 82, 85, 91; "Epitaph," 90–91; "Eros," 91; "Eurydice," 87–88, 157; "Fragment Thirty-six / *I know not what to do: / my mind is divided.* / Sappho," 89; "The Gift," 45, 114; "The God," 87; *Good Friend*, 142–43, 151; "Heat," 7, 45, 47, 156; *The Hedgehog*, 63–64, 154–55, 156, 157–58; *Hedylus*, 36–37, 38, 40, 45; *Heliodora*, 82, 83, 84, 86, 90, 156; "The Helmsman," 81, 82, 105; *HERmione*, 125, 128; *Hippolytus Temporizes*, 90; *Hymen*, 28, 89, 144, 156; influence of literary atmosphere on, 29; *Ion*, 157, 158; *Iphegenia* translation, 28; "I Said," 89; "The Islands," 82; "Let Zeus Record," 90; *The Majic Ring*, 109; "The Master," 2–3, 4–5, 91; *Mid-Day*, 145; "The Moon in Your Hands," 7; "Mouse Island," 109–10; and nature, 81–82; *Niké*, 109; and Niké image, 50; *Notes of Thought and Vision*, 107–9, 112; "Notes on Recent Writings," 117; "Not Honey," 89; "Orchard," 7; "Oread," 7, 45, 47, 82; and palimpsest image, 64; and patriarchal symbols, 64–65; "Peartree," 7; "The Poet," 1, 5–6, 92–93; *Poetry*, 89; and power of words, 151–52; "Projector," 111–12; "Pygmalion," 157; *Red Roses for Bronze*, 90, 145; *Sagesse*, 7–8, 45, 46; Sapphic fragments, 157; *Sea Garden*, 80, 81, 104–5, 156; "Sea Gods," 80, 105; "Sea Iris," 80; "Sea Lily," 156; "Sea Poppies," 80; "Sea Rose," 80; "Sea Violet," 80; *Selected Poems of H. D. (1957)*, 9; "She Contrasts with Herself Hippolyta," 28; "Sheltered Garden," 80; "The Shrine," 105; "The Tribute," 159; tripod image in, 19, 21, 65; use of signs in, 25; *Vale Ave*, 45; *Winter Love (Espérance)*, 45, 54–56, 60, 126

H. D.'s writings, characteristics of: creation of worlds in, 10; critical neglect of, 10, 45–49; deserted women in, 28–29, 44, 82–84; double meanings in, 65; experience of darkness in, 8; female perspective in, 48, 54–57, 65, 79; Freudian criticism of, 49–51, 53, 56–57, 64, 65; Freud's influence on, 47, 86–87; Greek mythology in, 23, 29, 43, 46–47, 82–86, 110–11; opposing forces in, 80, 89; past and present in, 8, 33, 37–38; phanopoeia in, 104–5, 110; poetry as prayer in, 105; problems of women writers in, 60; projection in, 102–7, 110; quest for female maturation in, 63; repetition in, 90; separate selves in, 35; sexist criticism of, 52–54, 59–60; sexuality in, 84, 144–46; static imagery in, 37–38; transparent mode in, 9; value of, 60–61; women heroes in, 60

Hedyle (*Hedylus*), 36–37

Hedylus (*Hedylus*), 36

Heilbrun, Carolyn, 57

Helen Fairwood (*Palimpsest*). See Fairwood, Helen

Helen in Egypt, 10, 45, 53, 123, 141–42; biographical basis for characters in, 124–29, 131, 132, 138; and Corfu vision, 101; as death-hymn, 127, 134, 138; as epic, 123–24; female values in, 57–58; hieroglyph in, 15; illumination in, 134–36; past and present in, 134;

180   INDEX

Three Powers, The (Burkhardt), 142
Towards a Recognition of Androgyny
     (Heilbrun), 57
Tribute to Freud, 28, 29, 33, 45–46,
     91; chalice image in, 19, 21; Corfu
     vision in, 19–21; criticism of, 49;
     fluid images in, 18–19; free asso-
     ciation in, 11–21; Gorgon's head
     image in, 19, 20; H. D.'s relation-
     ship with Freud in, 115; limita-
     tions of, 1–2; mythological
     associations in, 11–21; projection
     in, 116; psychic visions in, 107,
     109–10, 113; as psychobiography,
     26; tripod image in, 19, 21, 65
Tribute to the Angels. See Trilogy
Trilogy, 7, 22, 45, 65–78, 93–99, 142;
     Christian imagery in, 73–74, 75,
     95–96; and Corfu vision, 101; cre-
     ative power in, 96–97; criticism
     of, 52; crossroads image in, 160;
     darkness in, 8; female in, 57–58,
     64–65, 68, 76–77; goddess sym-
     bols in, 70–71, 74; happy mood
     in, 98; healing in, 76–77, 98–99;
     jar image in, 75; Lady image in,
     57, 73–74, 76, 97–98, 121, 143,
     144; opening images in, 94–95;
     past and present in, 72, 77; phano-
     poeia in, 110; poem as crucible in,
     120–21; power of words in, 150;
     redefinition in, 65, 71–73; rod im-
     age in, 68, 73, 96; sexuality in,
     146; shell image in, 65–68, 72;
     spatial imagery in, 65; storyteller
     in, 158–59; transmutation in, 116,
     117–22; transparent mode in, 9;
     war in, 78, 93–94, 96, 117, 118,
     120; worm imagery in, 68–69, 71

Van der Leeuw, J. J., 12
Vane (*Bid Me to Live*), 40, 43, 44
Van Eck, Peter, 109–10
Verrus (*Palimpsest*), 30, 34, 35

Waelder, Robert, 25
Wagner, Linda Welshimer, 53
Walls Do Not Fall, The. See Trilogy
War Trilogy. See Trilogy
Wilhelm Meister (Goethe), 14
Williams, William Carlos, 46, 48, 53,
     123; on H. D., 81–82, 156; and
     power of words, 151–52; vision
     of, 135, 136
Wing Beat, 111
Women: and bisexuality, 4; and criti-
     cism, 48–54, 59–61; deserted, 28–
     29, 30–31, 44, 82–83; friendships
     of, 30; and goddess images, 70–
     71, 74; modern experience of, 79;
     and mystery, 69–70; and patriar-
     chal symbols, 63–65, 66, 68, 70;
     perspective of, 48, 54–59, 76–77;
     quest for maturation of, 63; shell
     as symbol of, 68; and work, 58,
     59–60; worm as symbol of, 68–70
Wordsworth, William, 67
"Writing on the Wall." *See* Corfu vi-
     sion; *Tribute to Freud*

Yeats, W. B., 4, 26, 53

Zeus (*Helen in Egypt*), 127